TO YEATON
OUR EMILY "SAVIOUR"
AND CHRISTMAS COMPANION 1991 !

Bermuda's Favourite Haunts

VOLUME ONE

John Cox, Mac Musson and Joan Skinner welcome
you to this collection of tales from the other side
of yesterday. Steeped in the history of our own
unique environment, they are an intrinsic part of
Bermuda's heritage.

John Cox

Mac Musson

BOO !

Joan Skinner

Bermuda's Favourite Haunts

VOLUME ONE

Ghosted by John Cox, Mac Musson and Joan Skinner

To George Underwood. He understood.

Produced by:
The Boston Mills Press
132 Main Street
Erin, Ontario N0B 1T0
(519) 833-2407
Fax: (519) 833-2195

Typography and Design by Lexigraf, Tottenham, Ontario
Typestyles used: Belwe and Tekton
Cover Design by Gillian Stead, Guelph, Ontario
Printed by Ampersand, Guelph, Ontario

Published by Ghost Writers, P.O. Box FL 355, Flatts, Bermuda

Contents

Acknowledgements

To David L. White who said he actually had fun editing our first drafts, to Sheilagh Head for getting into the spirit of things, to Will Zuill who has kindly endorsed yet another facet of Bermuda's history, to Anthea Cox who opened her home and let the sun shine in, to Chris Wilcox, whose practised eye transformed Sheilagh's painting into slides for the printer, to Suzie Pewter whose enthusiasm directed us, to Kim Carter for introducing us to John Denison of The Boston Mills Press, to David Ashdown, the catalyst who brought the Ghostwriters together, and finally, to all those whose spirits are raised in the reading.

Cover: Devonshire Dock, from the original painting by Sheilagh Head
Colour slide for reproduction by Chris Wilcox
Pen, ink and pencil sketches by Mac Musson

References: 1966 through 1979
Royal Gazette, Mid-Ocean News, Bermuda Pictorial, Bermudian Magazine, Bermuda News Bureau,
Terry Tucker's Bermuda and the Supernatural

Foreword

by Will Zuill

This is a cheerful book about ghosts. The authors have reason to respect the unexplained, and together have compiled a most remarkable series of tales about inexplicable occurrences – inexplicable, that is, unless you believe in ghosts. At the same time, though, the authors give their tales in such a cheery way that the hair does not stand on end, one does not go into cold patches, and the cat does not howl as she sits on your lap – except, perhaps, to demand attention when you would rather continue your reading.

It is interesting that not everyone who lives in the houses described is aware of an unworldly presence, which bears out Nandor Fodor's contention that a person or family have to be in a certain psychological state of mind to see ghosts. The state of mind can be one of complete control, for nearly everyone has known utterly sober and sensible people who have seen ghosts.

I remember a tale from Britain told to me by an American friend. She was at a ladies' luncheon, and one of the ladies said to another:

"Are you still troubled by those monks?"

"Oh my, yes," said the other. "It was so hot last night we had to open the windows, and then we couldn't sleep, because they chanted every office."

The conversation went on in this vein for some time, and gradually my American friend realised that the monks were ghosts chanting in the ruins of an ancient monastery.

Most remarkable of all ghosts are the poltergeists who are able to fling things about or hide things. These occurrences are known to entire families – sometimes to neighbourhoods – and are the most difficult experiences to explain.

Most of us have never seen a ghost. Some would really like to, are utterly curious about this phenomenon, while others think it might be interesting, others are scared, and the remainder pooh-pooh the entire idea. That means there's something in this book for nearly all of us, with the added attraction that it gives glimpses of curious aspects of our island life, past and present.

So turn off the electric lights, settle down with a candle, put some slightly weird music on the phonograph, make sure you have a glass of something comforting beside you, and enjoy . . . .

Welcome to this collection of tales from the other side of yesterday. Steeped in the history and our own unique environment, they are an intrinsic part of Bermuda's heritage.

Bermuda's Favourite Haunts

Chuang Tsu – "Birth is not a beginning. Death is not an end."

Dare we hope you were lulled into picking up this book because to you a Favourite Haunt might suggest a merry chain of pubs filled with bonhommie, frivolous enjoyment and lusty gossip? . . . . In other words, a handy reference guide to endless vistas of "happy hours" wherein the senses meet in pleasant profusion and eventual confusion. Shame upon us then, for our spirits don't come contained in glass vessels or wooden barrels. Neither cherubic genie nor bottle of djin have we!

How do we begin? In the beginning of course – but where is that exactly when we are dealing with nether regions: the world of shadows and myth, fallacy, imagination, superstition, truth or fiction and just plain old lies. The nucleus must be there if there is a story to be told. The world of intangibles that, for reasons unknown, take brief form. That chink of light in the darkness unexpectedly illuminating a moving tableau from the past, giving it an instants reality before it recedes once more into the now popularly accepted "Twilight Zone".

Are you ready? Will you join us for a visit to a different aspect of Bermuda's centuries-old background? Share with us the tales of myriad emotions caught in the web of a time warp . . . the 'Other Time', the storage house of past recall that remains to jog our ancient memory and enrich our living for better or worse. Love, hate, sadness, joy, and benevolence share space with anger, murder, despair, theft and piracy, forever renewing themselves, surviving time's passage and sharing a celebration of awareness with those whose sensitivities exist on a sympathetic historical wavelength.

St. Anne's Rectory, Southampton

Recounted by Mrs. Reginald Harvey, widow of Canon Harvey, to Joan Skinner

After our marriage I moved into the St. Anne's Rectory with Reg. It is a very old house with many interesting features including a bricked-up and plastered-over fireplace, which is said to have a secret passage.

There were many strange noises at night, doors opening and shutting, footsteps etc., and when I asked Reg about them, he said airily "Oh yes, the place is haunted; Canon Walker (a predecessor who lived in the house for many years, and who started Somers College there) often visits us at night. I see him and talk to him . . . ."

Seeing the horror on my face, he quickly added, "but he is very friendly, nothing to be frightened of."

The noises and footsteps continued, and then one night I distinctly heard Reg speaking to someone. Next morning I asked him about this and he replied that he couldn't sleep and had gone to have a chat with Canon Walker.

"Next time he visits" I said bravely, "wake me up; I want to see this gentleman."

A few nights later, Reg woke me and said softly, "He's here."

There in the doorway, the bedroom door was never closed, stood a man.

"Describe him to me," said Reg, "then I'll know you really can see him."

Without hesitation I said, "He's tall, has silver-grey hair, longer than usual, he's got a stiff clerical collar, something black, and he's wearing a long white alb – under his arm is a black book."

"That's him to a tee," said Reg, then, "Meet Canon Wa . . ." Before he got any further, I let out a yell and flew into Reg's bed. With that wicked chuckle of his, he said, "My! We must do this more often!" – and I swear I saw a smile on Canon Walker's face.

The bumps and noises continued and I got used to them, but I never saw Canon Walker again.

Reg said he did, frequently, and I believed him. When Reg retired from St. Anne's, we went to live in St. George's, and I'm happy to say that Canon Walker did not accompany us!

Winton in Devonshire

by Mac Musson

Over 200 years ago a pattern for future haunting developed in the myriad lives of those about whom this story revolves. Capt. John Dill wed Christiana Love and built a home for his wife and family and called it Winton. A stalwart individual, John Dill was a merchant seaman and Master of his merchant sailing vessel.

To Christiana, a lady of great character who bore the burden of second sight, went the lonely role of mistress of the household, and manager of the small estate. In those days it was natural for a seafarer's family to keep a daily lookout for sightings of departing and, especially, returning ships, for such was the highlight of the day for all the islanders – it meant food, clothing and news from other shores and the safe return of loved ones.

It was not unusual, on moonless nights, to see a light, a beacon swaying in the wind, sending its message to the outer darkness to show the way . . . this same ghostly light can be seen to this day, on occasion, by passersby, dancing up and down the welcoming arm steps of Winton.

This reflection from the distant past bears witness to the watchful constancy of those who have their men at sea. Thus it was on every stormy night, even more so on this night when her forebodings finally bore fruit.

As the north winds chilled the weather side of Winton, rattling the door with insistent force, she ran to it and flung it open, only to gasp in shocked disbelief. Tom, her son-in-law stood there, dripping water and seaweed onto the top step and gazing in unspoken regret as he dissolved into fragmented salt spray and blackness. She slammed the door to hold back the night, but it couldn't hold back the despair that overwhelmed her.

Her daughter's husband!

It had happened all over again. She knew he had drowned just like her son John had, 21 years before!

Inside, her daughter was labouring to bring new life into the world. How could she tell her that her husband would never return? Christiana held her own counsel and maintained a stoic silence. The months passed without word, and the truth could no longer be avoided.

The sea around us bears no malice, and grants no favors in its claims upon life. Months passed as the realization slowly seeped in against all denial – Captain Thomas Dill, his crew, and sailing vessel, had slipped out of time and into history.

Who would have imagined the turn of events that were to transpire when we signed the lease for Winton? The history of Winton was unknown to us and its singular peculiarities were yet to impress themselves on us. Obviously the house was respectably old having been built in the mid 1700s. The interior was in many respects, quite gracious in an unpretentious way – old Bermuda in every respect including cedar woodwork. The old brick ovens and kitchen fireplaces and a semi-crude basement that hinted at servants' quarters next to air spaces and storage rooms and, through a small aperture, another room which proved to be a sad relic of the past . . . a cell that had held in chains the mentally disturbed Indian slave, who, in a fit of rage, had attempted to axe his master. Appalled, the mistress of the house, seeing what was about to happen, moved quickly to deflect the wild aim of the demented man and in the ensuing tussle he was subdued and then confined, for his own safety as well as others.

In winter it was cold as any Bermuda stone house can be, set high on the North Shore over-looking the sea – but cold within cold is another matter! A standing coldness has its own character, holding its breath as it draws heat from your personal warmth. A presence without menace, it was simply THERE, like a cold question mark or a frozen "hello".

And so it was that we became aware of not being alone. It had been a brief introduction, soon to be followed by a gentle camaraderie, demanding our attention more and more as time went on.

In a scientific manner we determined that these patches of cold were not naturally accountable. One evening, the reliable old cigarette smoke test resulted in the smoke gently spiralling upwards as if in a vacuum . . . BUT . . . only within that confined area of intense cold. Elsewhere in the room the smoke properly reacted to the pull of oxygenated air being drawn towards a roaring fire. Enough, we thought, and took our slightly bemused selves off to bed.

Two normal nights followed. Then we were treated to a second visitation.

We had bypassed a relaxing evening by the fire and retired to bed with a sturdy kerosene stove belting out warmth three feet to the left side of a double bed. This time the cold patch inserted itself between us and the heat and, once again, being chain smokers in those days, we wondered at the smoke rising tranquilly to the ceiling eliminating the slightest hint of any drafts. Puzzling, but hardly

alarming. Still, it's funny how people cease to look one another in the eye when something of this nature shakes previous convictions to bits.

Later that night, the dog took off! We don't mean he ran away. On the contrary, dear George was devoted to his family and was a champion watchdog. Whatever it was that hovered at the foot of the bed in the darkness, George displayed his total objection in no uncertain terms. He growled, barked and lunged at the foot of the bed repeatedly. George was not a lap dog, nor a dog that opted to sleep on the bed. He liked his privacy too, and preferred the corner of the room or a nearby armchair for his nightwatch. Only when our new-found spirit approached did George make for the bed and begin his ghost-defying antics.

As soon as I had uttered what became a more or less weekly password to peace and quiet, "Christiana! Don't mess around!", there would be a pause while George satisfied himself that all was once again as it should be, resuming his perch for the rest of the night.

Such was the pattern for things to come and, though they varied from time to time, from wall-tapping and swishing taffeta, to double-door closures being reversed, it was clear we were on the path of a relationship that was to annoy and entertain us for ten out of the eleven months of our tenancy.

In the end, it was more like three shadowed beings intruding their personalities into our daily routine. Mood variations from inquisitive to capricious to lonely permeated our consciousness.

To have sympathetic mental acceptance in a haunted household must be the staff of etheric life! In any event, our family had increased by at least one, judging from the various grumblings and oaths of frustration that went the rounds each day . . . things were forever being 'found' missing or moved elsewhere!

It was primarily Christiana to whom we addressed our comments, since she was the recognized and accepted resident ghost and perpetrator of dubious deeds.

Having come to terms with the fact that not all the happenings at Winton were going to be of a corporeal nature, we settled into a routine of wry "normalcy." Christiana's need for companionship found many ways of insinuating itself into our social structure. So it came about, if any guests were new to our invisible "freezing unit", that the little cold spot also attended, moving from visitor to visitor as if to give them its personal attention. Indeed, our little cold spot seemed to drift according to the conversational source. Nor did George try to snitch the brownies from the tray if "it" was hovering nearby – he always did otherwise!

Many adult Bermudians will remember Sister Jean De Chantal Kennedy; others will know her through her books about Bermuda. For her there was no barrier to the unknown and the paranormal. She was psychic and a sensitive and therefore broached no opposition to the tentative suggestion that there might be a world of spirits. So it was that to Sister Jean went an almost custom-tailored experience on a day of the Queen's official birthday celebration at Government House.

It was Sister Jean who suggested we go together. As I readied myself with despised hat and white gloves, the phone rang. Deborah, my 10 year old, ran to answer it but it stopped ringing before she could reach it. She had barely returned to the family room when it resumed its summons. I could hear the conversation in the distance. Later, in the car, Sister Jean said, "When I rang the first time a young girl answered the phone and said it was Winton but it was NOT the Musson home and immediately hung up on me! It was like walking past myself when I redialled, the scenario a rerun, only this time it was Deborah giving me all the right answers."

Needless to say, we were all intrigued at the obvious implication and even impressed at the audacity of spiritus matter taking a stand as to whose house Winton really was! Upon returning home, I stood in the hallway and told Christiana a thing or two about who was paying the rent!

Deborah Musson Hollis:

"I was nine years old when we moved into Winton and, at that time, I don't recall ever having dwelled upon ghosts or goblins except at Hallowe'en. I can't point out any specific time or place for realizing Winton was not a normal house, it seemed a natural process with no real knowledge of where or when . . . simply a gradual sense of being a part of WHATEVER it was and feeling quite natural with WHOMEVER it was.

I remember going into town with my mother to get paint. I distinctly recall Mr. Jim Zuill serving my mother and as he made out the charge for Winton, asking her, "Have you met the ghost yet?"

This was our first real indication that what we had experienced was not all in our heads – for none of us had HONESTLY believed in ghosts before.

On a night six months into our stay, I remember waking without warning, my eyes drawn to the area where the fireplace was, and there, just above it and directly below the cedar beam in the ceiling, was a face! . . . Looking at me! . . . Staring! I was unable to move. As I watched her I soon began to relax with the realization that it was our Christiana casting a benign and kindly gaze on me.

Knowing I was face to face with a "friend" I turned at last, pulling the covers over my head saying – "GOODNIGHT Christiana!" With that I slept contentedly 'til morning and upon rising, hurried to tell my mother what had transpired.

The next night I awoke suddenly again and blinked my eyes several times in amazement as I watched the same Christiana glide away from the door adjoining my mother's room, past my bed, and disappear through the closet wall separating the bedroom and dining room. I either fell back to sleep or passed out, in any event I knew no more until morning.

In retrospect I can't remember my exact feelings during these events but I don't think I felt fear since I continued to sleep in my room soundly and without concern every night thereafter until we moved. Mostly I think I just felt surprise that this friendly household companion took the chance of frightening me with this rather theatrical demonstration that would live on in my memory. But maybe THAT was what she wanted, after all."

Back to Mac:

After the movers had transferred the contents of our household to Inland, in Pembroke, I returned to Winton to complete the cleaning. As I proceeded to clean and oil the wood floors, starting with the bedrooms and the entrance hall, which for so many nights past had held the sounds of rustling taffeta and wall tapping – to the living and dining rooms, where temperatures fluctuated madly, I was followed by loud and insistent footsteps. Back and forth, around, pause, staying with me, as if we were dancers performing a confused minuet. A mockery of movement or a last frantic appeal?

A brooding and speculative stillness had prevailed on my first introduction to Winton a year before. No noisy bouncing floorboards, no echoes then . . . no nothing. I could not liken what was happening to anything I'd experienced before. So it was, as I quickly completed my final cleaning, I backed toward the kitchen door taking my broom and mop with me and uttering for the last time a fond, "Goodbye Friends, you're not to follow us, please!" . . . . pulled the halfdoor after me and was gone.

I have never returned, though when I see glimpses of the house with its "silent" exterior, I think back and – wonder.

Other People – Other Times, at Winton

Jim Zuill, brother of Ann Williams, the owner of Winton, is quoted as saying he had often heard footsteps that seemed to follow him from room to room during the time he resided there, and Mr. Leslie Young was convinced that someone stood behind him watching over his shoulder to see what he was doing. In the Mussons' book at least, Christiana & Company were found to be decidedly pokey and, on occasion, downright interfering. Jim Zuill wryly recalls another moment shared with the eternal lady of the house. He was busily engaged in catching up on bills and accounts at the desk by the dining room window – it was early evening and he was alone in the house. Concentration has a knack of separating a person from his immediate surroundings and it was in this frame of mind he was suddenly made aware of the sound of the dining room chair behind him making its usual scraping noise when moved. With this prickly realization came that good old "moment of truth" as he turned to see the chair was now angled as if to accommodate a seated visitor.

On yet another occasion, the "benevolent one" entered the bedroom, then occupied by two startled ladies. They sat and watched in disbelief as the greyish presence set herself down on the bed for several moments before wafting off to perform some errand in the great beyond.

Mary Margaret Dill found herself at odds with supernature during a family gathering at Winton. She came out of the bathroom and noticed the cupboard door hanging open, barring her way. It wouldn't close properly so she looked in to see if something had fallen. She was nudged inside, the door promptly shut and, if you please, bolted!

Since a family party was gathered in the living room, it was some time before her husband noticed she hadn't returned from powdering her nose. Excusing himself, he wandered to the back of the house in search of her, and was suddenly aware of a muffled string of oaths emanating from the area of the bathroom.

Mary Margaret continued to swear for some time after being released, since she was sure someone had fun and games at her expense. No one there owned up to such a prank and, in fact, there was no one there who could be even considered a likely candidate for that kind of tomfoolery.

The children were off to school so, alone at last and able to relax, Mary Tucker, thinking she was alone, took a bath and, in minutes, wished she hadn't. No sooner was she steeped in the warm bubbly water than there began a series of light tappings on the bathroom door, followed by an insistent female voice calling her name:

"Mary!" "Who's that?"

"Mary!" "Who are you, dammit, I'm all wet!"

"Mary! Oh, Mary!" "Oh, all right, I'm coming."

"Mary!!"

Mary remembers: "Pestilence! Out I get, grab a towel and open the door . . . who's there? No one! I dash out through the hall and dining room to the kitchen . . . not a soul in sight . . . inside or out!"

Her husband Brian, a no-nonsense hardliner, took to keeping a piece of pipe under the bed because of the strange sounds from below. Was it a break-in or was it just the house acting up again? He swore chains were being dragged around the basement and somehow felt threatened by the sound.

Thomasina and Desmond Fountain, Sr. had many experiences at Winton . . . as with the Mussons, all were interesting, none frightening.

Hiding articles seems to be one of the prime attention getters of these ethereal household pests.

Tommy says: "The face cream I had only just bought and put in my dresser drawer disappeared almost immediately and was found by accident a few days later in the unused antique bread oven which was built into the wall of most old Bermuda homes.

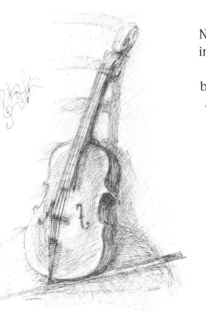

"Then there was the violin. We had musical evenings all by ourselves with Desmond playing his violin accompanied by a phonograph record. At the conclusion of one of these mini-concerts, it was obvious that either the record or the violin was off key. If it was the record player, then there was a problem involving parts and labour, if only the violin, then it could be tuned later.

Setting the instrument aside they forgot about it for the moment. As the evening drew to a close, the silence was shattered by the sounds of the "A" string being plucked and, if you please, the violin was sitting there in the hall chair trying to tune itself!

"On another occasion, since we enjoyed music in our home and featured it greatly in our hours of relaxation, it was as if Christiana had this in mind when, as the first side ended, the record-player obligingly turned itself onto the other side as I listened from the kitchen, my hands immersed in soapy water as I washed dishes.

"Talk about having a fairy at the bottom of the garden! It was wonderful to have this service performed for me but in the final analysis I had to admit to a certain amount of wry perplexity, since, after having heard it through to its finale, I went to the player only to find it was still on side one."

More recently, a visitor to the house, whose tenants were happily unaware of any extra residents, strolled into the hallway and was transfixed in wonder as he gazed at some unannounced arrivals who seemed to be quietly engrossed in their own concerns. The uninvited group consisted of a black manservant, judging by his attire, an elegantly dressed white lady, and two children. As the startled visitor approached them, they faded and were gone. Somewhat taken aback, the house guest was reluctant to discuss the incident with his hosts at first, but some time later did finally tell them of his experience. The family was intrigued but, for them, there was never an unusual incident to mull over. Winton always had had a friendly feel about it for them, although they did comment on the fact that, in retrospect, there was a section of the basement that they always avoided without being quite sure why.

Many a night a lantern would be seen gliding up and down the steep front steps at Winton, held aloft by unseen hands. The Grey Lady, a regular in those parts, has been known to impose her presence on the unsuspecting, playing games of "now you see me, now you don't" between Winton, Parson's Lane, and the old Devonshire Churchyard. It has become an accepted pattern for Christiana Love Dill who continues to oversee the family estates, and her descendants. She is part of the history of old Devonshire.

Some in-house ghosts don't have much regard for other residents and, after the Fountains left Winton, one spirited "reject" got a tad bloody minded, seeming not to fancy the new tenant at all. In fact, one entity got rather offish about it. Its resentment was justified, as it turned out, for it was this tenant who caused all the disembodied regulars to be banished and shelved on the outskirts of time, sent there by a professional exorcist.

The entities that "would", are held in suspended silence . . . for now. As to how lasting these restrictions are, only time will tell, but who can play the waiting game better than they?

Sherlock in Devonshire

by John Cox

Across from Orange Valley is a very old house called Sherlock, which was built in the 1730s by Samuel Sherlock, a prominent justice in the Parish.

One day, Judge Sherlock and his family were seated around the gateleg table in the hall reading the Bible when, suddenly, from the upstairs parlour came a small cry followed by the sound of a little bump on the floor. The family quickly rushed upstairs to investigate, and found Judge Sherlock's youngest daughter lying on the cedar floor, shivering violently. The little girl was helped to bed and the doctor called. Nothing could be done, for it was the dreaded typhoid, and after three days of terrible suffering, the poor girl died.

Observations by Deborah Hollis and her brother, John Musson:

Deborah: "Perhaps that accounts for the strange goings-on we encountered when my husband Charles and I first lived in the old house. On many evenings at about dusk, when we were sitting in the living room after a busy day, we would be startled by the sound of a child singing quietly to herself upstairs, and at intervals, the patter of light footsteps.

"Now we had, in effect, returned to the home territory of Christiana Love Dill and those strong family connections, and it was clearly not beyond our imaginations to ponder the likelihood of her identifying with us once more. Would she pick up on our vibrations or had we grown away from such impressionistic associations?

"It was many years since Winton, but as memory can act as a trigger, we might as well clear the air right now. If anything WAS there at Sherlock, it was not Christiana and, since we had no reason to believe this house was haunted, it was only its age that made it suggestively promising. The word "suggestive" would appear to be the key to our impressions, however, as with Winton, we had no fore-knowledge concerning the history of the old place or the people who had lived in it.

"In due course our first daughter, Sara, was born. We had already become wryly accustomed to the sound of little feet pattering across the floor above us therefore, although it occasionally bore looking into, we more or less ignored it. Infants don't run around, do they? Later when we knew her to be capable of letting herself out of her crib we would be forced to run up and check on her activities – there were none since she usually slept like the dead once succumbing to a child's total and healthy exhaustion.

"The sounds continued as Sara grew, with laughter and singing becoming a part of the whole, and eventually, she moved to her big bed in anticipation of the new brother or sister who would soon be sharing the room with her. For a time, the overhead thumps took on a different meaning since they were followed by a wail as Sara fell out of bed one more time.

"Her childish chatter after lights out was a nightly occurrence. No one thought anything of it until little snatches of speech developed, imparting the great news that "naughty, little elves" played in her room at night and stopped her from sleeping. They would come through "the door" and play with her toys and laugh at her. "The door" was to the closet and we knew it had opened originally on to the old stone stairway that circled down to the living room. Everyone loves a secret place and this became the mysterious "walled up" area – a delicious idea for the imaginative. Sara ceased falling out of her bed and Alexandra arrived. The room was more than ever alive with anticipation. Another playmate on the scene!"

John: "When I agreed to house-sit while they all went to England for two weeks, I had no idea of the history of the house and had been there only a couple of nights when, worn out after a long day at work, I retired early to the master bedroom. I fell into a deep sleep and suddenly found myself wide awake. Partially rising and opening my eyes, my groggy mind recorded a startling fact. I was not alone! A small girl was standing by my bed, clutching a rag doll or stuffed animal of sorts. She gazed at me intently, shaking her head back and forth as if to deny my presence. I turned away and then looked back in disbelief . . . she was still there, somewhat luminous and clearly disapproving of my intrusion. Swearing to myself and now, somewhat alarmed, I reached out for the bedside lamp and quickly switched it on. There was nothing there but a faint disturbance in the air, as if a shadow had flickered past. I promptly left the room, taking a blanket as I went, and spent the remainder of the house-sit sleeping on the living room couch. The placid family dog, now released from the confines of kitchen duty, curled happily nearby in comforting attendance."

John Cox concludes:

"Deborah and Charles had frequently, and with amusement, informed me (and as it turned out, John Musson had wished they'd informed him too!), that "as long as we keep the closet in the spare bedroom locked, we don't hear the invisible children. We have come to believe "she", and just possibly another playmate, inhabits the closet." Due to his ignorance of the matter, John later admitted to having left the closet door wide open after putting his clothes away."

Not far away, at the old Devonshire Parish Church, is a walled burial plot containing several graves. This wall was erected right against the Church in 1732 by Judge Sherlock, who is buried there along with his family. It was then boldly inscribed with the family coat-of-arms, but over the years this has become weathered and faded. Today, a wild Bermuda rose bush grows within the Sherlock burial plot and, at certain times of the year, it is very pretty with its delicate pink blossoms which droop mournfully over the graves after a spring rain.

Orange Valley

by John Cox

When a storm blows in from the northwest, and a sharp wind funnels between the hills which form a ridge above Orange Valley, the old house heaves and creaks and the windows rattle ominously.

Standing in the dimly lit hall, crowded with eighteenth century cedar chairs and the elegant grandfather clock which has stood in the house since the time it was built by my ancestor, Captain William Cox, in 1796, one is grippingly aware of the past. With the gale blowing outside, the atmosphere within the house seems alluring.

"There must be a ghost here!" says a visitor entering Orange Valley for the first time.

I answer blithely that there is.

The subject is rarely pursued because, in passing, I do not like to talk about the ghost. Although I have never seen it, I actually experienced it some years ago which caused me serious alarm. At the time, I was occupying the west bedroom upstairs. Night after night I was awakened by strange footsteps pacing back and forth across my room. Eerie lights would also pass by the opened door which led into the day room, and small objects on the bureau would move of their own accord.

Sometimes I would feel that I could not breathe, as though I were being choked. Finally, after many unnerving encounters, I called out loudly, "Please, whoever you are, stop this. You are frightening me!"

In the next instant I was aware of someone standing over me. A warm hand touched my neck. It was as real as if my own mother had touched me. After that night I was never again troubled by the ghost.

There are those who have SEEN the ghost, or perhaps I should say ghosts, at Orange Valley. One summer afternoon, some 20 years ago, a cousin brought her twin daughters to a young family member's birthday party. As my cousin was making her way back around the house to leave, she suddenly came upon a woman wearing a long, white dress. Her hair was pulled up behind her head.

"The mysterious woman seemed to want to communicate with me, but she said nothing," recounted my cousin. "She just gazed intently at me. She next beckoned me towards the old rose garden. I looked toward the garden, some 40 feet away, and then back at the mysterious woman, but she had vanished, as quickly as that! I knew then that I had encountered a ghost. For a while I had an odd feeling about it, but I tried not to let it bother me."

A hundred years ago, a spinster aunt named Laura Cox, lived at Orange Valley, and she took a special interest in growing roses. After her untimely death of palsy in 1861, the rose garden was left to overgrow with weeds. Could the mysterious apparition have been Aunt Laura? No one can say for certain.

Back in 1974, my youngest brother and a few of his friends pitched a tent on the extensive grounds around Orange Valley where they camped for a night. Returning to the house at dawn the following morning, the boys distinctly noticed a middle-aged man staring down at them from the south window of the east bedroom. Although there was sufficient light in the sky, the garden was still dim. My brother shone his torch on the mysterious man whose eyes gleamed as the light passed over them. He was portly and he wore a dark cloak. All of the boys saw him clearly. Soon after, he faded away. In the next instant my father was awakened and the upstairs rooms were thoroughly searched. No one was discovered.

Years later, when I was preparing a history of Orange Valley, I asked my grandfather why the south window of the east bedroom was much larger than the other windows in that room. My grand-

father explained that when he was a boy the room was partitioned. He slept in the northern half, while an eccentric uncle named Aubrey Cox used the southern half. Uncle Aubrey put the large window in because each morning he was in the habit of rising early so that he could stand at the window and watch the approaching dawn. Remembering the episode, my brother and his friends had related to the family years before, a chill ran down my spine!

Only recently, while conducting a tour of architectural students through Orange Valley, a young woman on the tour took me aside and said, "You will probably think me crazy, but do you know you have a ghost in the house?"

"Well, we have several," I answered.

"No, this is serious."

The woman clasped my arm tightly. She was clearly disturbed.

"I have communicated with the spirit of a woman of about 40 years of age. She says her name is Mary and she is very distressed because her husband is away at sea and he doesn't know she is ill."

Looking through the family genealogical records, I learned that Orange Valley's builder, Captain William Cox, had married a woman named Mary Robinson in 1790, who died of pneumonia at Orange Valley in April, 1806, aged only 42. At the time of her illness and death Captain Cox was sailing in the West Indies. I shuddered to think that the spirit of poor Mary Cox had been searching for her husband all these many years.

A large India rubber tree, planted by William Cox in 1847, marks the spot where the original drive to the house began. Sitting formidably upon its rising mound, the old Georgian-style house still reigns proudly over its garden of twisted palmettos and cedars. The past reflecting the continuum of lives intertwined through the tree of life . . . relatively speaking.

Palmetto House

by John Cox

One of Devonshire's oldest and finest houses is Palmetto House which lies east of Barker's Hill, off the North Shore Road. Built in the cruciform style about 1700, this was for generations the home of the Williams family. Palmetto House is built into a steep hill so that it is three stories in the front and one story at the back. It would have had casement windows originally, and probably a thatched roof of palmetto leaves. Inside are fine old cedar beams and rafters, along with a handsomely carved staircase and traces of half timbering on the upper floor. An old detached kitchen stands behind the house.

In the early nineteenth century Benjamin S. Williams was living at Palmetto House with his wife, Frances Cox and their five daughters. Mr. Williams was choirmaster and organist at Devonshire Church. He showed great kindness to several Canadian exiles who were sent to Bermuda by Lord Durham after the Papineau Rebellion in 1838, offering them his pew during Sunday services. The exiles were invited to join the Williamses at Palmetto House for musical entertainments. While one of the Williams girls played the piano, one of the exiles played a violin, and all sang along; their lovely voices permeating the still night air, illuminated only by the soft glow of candlelight. Many a passerby would stop and listen and marvel at the beautiful music coming from within the house.

The exiles returned to Canada late in 1838, leaving such mementoes behind them as a few romantic quotes on pink pages of albums, a sketch or two, and some small and treasured objects for the great kindnesses rendered them during their stay.

Benjamin S. Williams died at Palmetto House in 1843. His wife outlived him by many years. Late in life, Mrs. Williams took to enjoying afternoon siestas in an elaborate coffin which she stored beneath her fourposter bed. One afternoon, upon returning home from Flatts, Mrs. Williams found an old neighbourhood drunk sound asleep in her coffin. Aghast, she angrily shook him awake, saying "Get your own coffin to sleep in!"

The War Department, established at Prospect, took over Palmetto House late in 1867, and the eccentric Mrs. Williams was moved away to Hamilton, with all her possessions, including her coffin. She died in 1869 sleeping as peacefully in her coffin as she did in life.

Early in this century, when the War Department had no further use for Palmetto House, it was allowed to fall into disrepair, until historian, Parliamentarian and art collector, the Honourable Hereward T. Watlington came to the rescue and restored it for the Bermuda Historical Monuments Trust, predecessor of the Bermuda National Trust which now owns and rents Palmetto House.

Its first tenants were Polish refugees, Mr. and Mrs. André Bohomolec, who came to live here about 1946. They related that on several occasions they would be wakened at night by the sound of someone playing a piano in the drawing room below, though no such instrument at that time existed in that room or, indeed, in the house. This continued for many nights and always, upon investigation, no logical explanation could be provided. Finally the Polish couple ignored the disturbances and, eventually, the mysterious sounds of piano playing ceased altogether. However, some time later, the wife had a further brush with the supernatural which could not be dismissed as easily. One still, summer afternoon, as the wife returned from Hamilton and was making her way through the front of the house, she stopped suddenly at the sight of a young woman staring down the stairs at her from the landing above. The woman had ringlets and wore a long gray dress. After several moments the woman turned and walked through a small passage into the west bedroom. The wife quickly made her way upstairs and entered the bedroom. No trace of anyone could be found.

The wife never saw the young woman with her ringlets again but one December evening two children arrived at the front door carrying boxes of cookies for sale. They informed the wife that they had been greeted moments before at the foot of the welcoming arms steps by a pretty woman who, they felt, acted in a most peculiar way, and then walked away very abruptly around the house.

"What did she look like?" asked the wife.

"She had very funny hair," proclaimed the youngsters "and she wore a long, gray dress."

Could this mysterious young woman have been Miss Margaret Williams, the youngest daughter of Benjamin and Frances Williams, who grew up at Palmetto House during the 1840s, and who died before her twentieth birthday? There are no sure answers; a pen and ink sketch taken from her photograph provides only an enigmatic smile.

The present day tenants, Wing Commander and Mrs. E.M. Ware say that they have never seen or heard anything out of the ordinary at Palmetto House. Despite this, the atmosphere there seems perfect for harbouring the supernatural.

Perhaps the mysterious young woman is finally at rest or, just resting.

Footnote: André Bohomolec will be remembered by many older Bermudians for his wonderful pottery which he worked on in the back of Palmetto House while he and his wife lived there. It was André Bohomolec and artist, Antoine Verpilleaux who, together, created the Diorama at Fort St. Catherine, which is still a valued feature viewed daily by hundreds of visitors and locals alike.
Palmetto House is opened to the public, free of charge, every Thursday between the hours of 10 and 5 o'clock through the kindness of the Wares and the Bermuda National Trust.

The Grove

by John Cox

Another old house which is reputed to have been visited by ghosts is The Grove which is set amidst rolling hills in the middle of Devonshire Parish. Built in 1717 by Captain Richard Gilbert, a prominent ship-owner of the time, The Grove has always been lived in by Captain Gilbert's descendants, and through the many generations they have lovingly protected and preserved the old house. Inside, beautifully proportioned rooms are adorned with tray ceilings, and each morning, from the eastern windows, the sunlight gently reawakens the old-world atmosphere of the place.

Early one summer morning, back in 1950, my father and my grandmother were sitting at the breakfast table in the dining room of The Grove when they heard a horse and carriage pull up to the house and stop at the front door. The carriage brake came on and the horse snorted.

My father arose and went to greet whoever had arrived, but when he reached the door and looked out across the verandah, there was no one about, much less a horse and carriage.

Puzzled, my father returned into the house where his mother reassured him that she had also heard the carriage and went on to say, "I've heard the same horse and carriage on several occasions and I was beginning to think my hearing was playing tricks on me. But now I know that we really DID hear it."

Since the 1960s, when cars multiplied considerably on Devonshire's by-ways, the ghost carriage has not been heard arriving at The Grove. It must have been overwhelmed by all the modern traffic.

A couple of years ago, when a friend and I were alone at The Grove, we distinctly heard someone walking through the house. The footsteps paused for a few moments in the dining room, and then continued down the back corridor towards the sitting room. When we went to find who was there, however, no one answered. We were the only two people in the house, yet we both knew that we had heard a third person. It was very mysterious.

One night during the summer of 1982, a cousin was alone in the house when he heard similar footsteps which he could not account for, and several nights later, when my brother was asleep in the guest bedroom, he awoke to hear heavy footsteps pass his door and go down the corridor and into the library. My brother quickly went into the library to investigate, but there was no one there. I suppose when an old house, such as The Grove, has been lived in for so many years there are bound to be ghosts.

More than 150 years ago, the keel marks of the "Rosemary Ship" could be seen at The Grove, and, not long before that, rosemary grew thickly on the bank beneath the road where it had been growing as long as anyone could remember. The legend of the "Rosemary Ship" is part of the folklore of Devonshire Parish, where it has been told to generations of children since early days.

Once upon a time there was a Bermuda sea captain whose mother-in-law was reputed to be a witch. One year the captain had to go on a voyage to London and took his wife and mother-in-law with him. As soon as they reached London, they heard on all sides of a great scarcity of rosemary and of the high prices it would fetch if one was lucky enough to have any. One night, a few days later, the whole ship's company slept ashore, leaving on board the ship only the old woman and a young slave. The following morning, when the crew came on board, they were astonished to smell the pungent perfume of rosemary.

"What's this?" they cried. "This smells like rosemary!"

The slave boy, looking rather frightened, replied, "It is rosemary. Look in the hold, it's full of rosemary."

The men ran to the hatch, pulled off the cover, and gazed into the hold. It was true. The hold was full to the top with fresh, sweet-smelling rosemary.

"How did this get here?" they demanded.

"T'ole missus and me went to Bermuda last night and sailed all over the land and gathered it," confessed the lad.

But the old woman would say nothing, and, of course no one believed the boy, for how could a small sailing vessel go to Bermuda from London and return in a night? This had to be the first air-lift in mercantile history!

The rosemary sold for a high price, and the voyage turned out to be the most prosperous one the captain had ever had. At last they returned to Bermuda, and when they were all at home again, the old woman took the captain and his wife through the land to the rosemary bank and showed them the marks of the keel.

Admiralty House at Spanish Point

Reported to Mac Musson by Chan McIvor

Originally a private dwelling nestled on the crest of Clarence Hill, it was converted to the first official residence of the first Admiral to be appointed to this station in 1816. The outer buildings were constructed to provide suitable officers' quarters and mess which still stand today, now known as the Admiralty House Community Centre.

Once installed, the Admiral was known to patrol the premises in fair weather or foul, much as he would the bridge of his ship, and would frequently be seen raising his spyglass to the horizon from the stone deck of the house that faced the North Shore.

The old house itself, neglected for too long, had become ramshackle to the point of danger with rotting floorboards, and was subjected to controlled burning by the Fire Department in 1974. Residents still recall the old building that stood for nearly 200 years overlooking Clarence Cove in Spanish Point.

Bubbles Burnard, who recently passed away, was Quartermaster of the Bermuda Regiment for many years, and he and his wife lived at Admiralty House from 1962 until shortly before part of the rambling old house was destroyed. During their stay there were many nights when strange noises drew them from their beds. They would periodically see the shadow of a ghostly old-time mariner drifting through the main hall and wearing the Nelson-like regalia of days gone by.

The Burnards were not the only ones treated to this spectacle, for the groundsman, George Tucker, often saw him pass by and there were several visitors too, who reported concern that such an aged old salt should be allowed to wander around on his own in the dark, . . . 'make anybody think they'd seen a ghost, for Heaven's sake.'

Since the residential portion of house was razed to the ground, every-so-often it is said that the old boy can still be seen standing on what was left of the crumbling stone steps, spyglass raised and scanning the horizon for his fleet.

Clarence Cove beach itself is the final resting place of a young midshipman, who was either the victim of a killing fever or an act of violence by a murderous third part of a lovers 'triangle', so it has been hinted. Since there used to be a small infirmary for sick naval personnel nearby, the former suggestion seems to be the most likely. Unlike the old Admiral however, he, at least, seems to rest in peace on the water's edge . . . we think.

Inwood – Paget

As told to Mac Musson by Susan Curtis

Inwood is a lovely old Bermuda home and, like a few houses of that period, was of the cruciform design, the "head" of which always faced the north. It was built by a family named Jones in the early 1700s. A true family home, Inwood nourishes a warmth that casts kindly reflections on the lives that flourished within its walls. A contented atmosphere prevails at Inwood, for no one living there ever feels other than safe with the intimate awareness that seems to hold it together.

Susan Ingham Curtis never knew a moment's anxiety while she lived there. Even her children, as they grew, developed a fun loving rapport with the ever tolerant and protective presence that had always made itself felt and came to be accepted by those who lived there.

Susan herself regrets never having seen the phantom spirit even though she dearly wanted to. She was most envious of Carol Fleiger, who was frequently treated to the sight of a young Miss Jones gracefully floating down the stairs and melting into walls, caught in a time-path through her home for more than 200 years.

Susan says: "Because of Miss Jones we had many fun-filled instances with good old belly laughs accompanying the proceedings – the children, (toads they were!), took delight in manufacturing ghostly demonstrations for the benefit of those whose superstitious beliefs made them ideal scapegoats for these childish pranks, while taking poor Miss Jones' name in vain! They had learned the knack of adjusting the pendulum in the otherwise empty grandfather clock that stood on the landing. Once set up only a slight nudge from invisible hands above would cause a resounding din as the chime was struck!

"With the children having now mastered the manipulation of the old clock, you can begin to see the manner in which the stage was set for the next available evening when Craig and I were to be out.

"The unfortunate babysitter for the occasion, to her undying credit, never deserted her post though it took all her courage to stick it out! Beyond speech, once released from her duties upon our return, she agitatedly declared that someone else would pick up her "message" the next day, and departed without a backward glance. She never returned. I have never seen such pallor; one hears of people turning white overnight, but surely they refer to hair? Later, we determined the cause of her hasty retreat and did our best to make amends, but our efforts were in vain.

"Our black cat was another matter – a witch cat if ever there was one! She "saw" whole parades of phantom visitors – never doubt those eyes of hers, THEY watched their passing. Her mien was one of intense interest, and she would sit still and silent, clearly avoiding being stepped upon; stopping her ablutions only to observe the invisible passerby before resuming her personal toilet, all as a matter of course.

"Maddening that I could only feel the calm reassurance of our Lady Jones. To this day I feel deprived, as if I had been left out of a confidence in spite of my accepting the idea of her without reservation. Of course, we had the creaking stairs and, apart from the kids, that damn gutless clock did, every-so-often, strike a baffled chime for no known reason. When this happened, yon cat could be seen sitting up and paying close attention to the stairs as usual. Whatever she saw was always descending the stairs, one step at a time.

To the uninitiated, in Bermudian parlance 'message' means the transfer of monies for services rendered.

35

More recently, Dr. Delmont Simmons, who now resides with his family at Inwood, amusedly recalled an anecdote concerning the following sequence of events that took place shortly after moving in to the main house.

With a major portion of the Inwood condominiums still under construction, Dr. Simmons and his wife, Marilyn, assumed they were the only inhabitants in the immediate area.

Similarly, Horst Augustinovic, and his wife, Heidi, assumed they were the sole residents of the Inwood Condominium complex, having been the first family to settle into the development in its early stages. Naturally enough, thinking themselves safe from observation, Heidi had felt her privacy was assured, and so, very early in the morning, dressed only in her flowing white nightgown, she took her small dog out to water the flower beds.

It seems that on the same morning, the newly arrived Dr. Simmons was standing at his kitchen window, enjoying the cool and peaceful atmosphere of his new surrounds, and sipping his coffee in quiet contemplation.

Suddenly, a vision in long flowing white came gliding across his line of vision, moving silently to the end of the property and disappearing.

We are not saying Dr. Simmons choked on his coffee, but it would not have been surprising if he had. After all, when one thinks they are the only living residents in a given area with a history of past hauntings, it would be quite understandable if, for a brief moment, Dr. Simmons had thought he'd "seen the ghost of Inwood."

Bloomfield

As told to Mac Musson by Ethel Gosling

I stood in rapt attention as I listened to Ethel Gosling one summers night in 1966 at Bloomfield in Paget. The story of Nancy Nelmes was a sad one which was recited in great detail and with much empathy and affection. The young woman "took a chill" and, as her wedding day approached, died. Nancy was repeatedly heard, sometimes weeping in the room that had been hers, and was frequently seen by a variety of people. Since Ethel ran Bloomfield as a guest house for a few years, there came a day when the friendly advances of Nancy's phantom were taken amiss and a newly arrived young bride was startled on the stairs as she felt a firm hand resting on her shoulders as if her attention was being sought. Surprised at the friendly warmth of the touch, she turned to see who it was. No one was to be seen! Observing this one-sided exchange, it was then that Ethel finally accepted the fact that she would have to forego the pleasure of her invisible resident, to whom the whole family had become so attached over the years. It was with the greatest regret that she secured the help of the clergy and arranged for an exorcism to be performed. So off went Nancy to her release and, we trust, welcoming new horizons.

The Nelmes family sold Bloomfield to the Goslings in the 1860s and moved across the way to the Deanery, which overlooks the Bloomfield estate. From here, it was said, the Nelmes daughters would gaze back with longing at the lushness and beauty of Bloomfield, regret at their loss uppermost in their hearts.

Mal and Mary Gosling took up residence at Bloomfield 22 years ago. During one lively family gathering, Mary wondered aloud to a cousin known for her sensitivity, "I wonder what Nancy Nelmes thinks of all these children running around?"

"She's out in the garden and very happy," was the reply.

Ethel had another tale to recount. This was not a haunting tale but rather one of a "precognitive visitation or crisis apparition" if you prefer.

With the weekend upon them all, Ethel and another friend had gone ahead to a picnic site upon the hilltop overlooking the sea, to await their three other chums. After some time, they were pleased to see the three tardy ones approaching. They were all waving happily to one another. Ethel and her friend above and the three making their way up from below. Five minutes and more passed as the distance closed between them . . . one quick look seaward at the sailboats beginning a race and the church bell began to toll. As they returned their attention to their friends, they realized there were only two of them. George had disappeared from view . . . .

"Where did George go?"

"George? He isn't coming, he's been home sick all week".

"But he was with you coming up the hill, we both saw him!"

"Well, you were both seeing things!"

"No we were NOT!"

Feeling each was playing tricks upon the other they challenged one another on and off for the rest of the afternoon.

When they reached home their parents informed them that George had passed away earlier that day, having lost his battle with pneumonia.

Government House

Researched by Mac Musson

I t has been suggested that one of our early Governors was so unpleasant that his wife was subjected to physical abuse and, probably, mental as well. Far be it for this writer to assert this as fact and defame the man's reputation further, however, the wife has been encountered haunting the grounds as if seeking the swine, clearly with a view to getting her own back.

Picture, if you will, a black-shrouded form with arms outstretched, a pale face and dark circles in place of searching, woeful eyes, looking for the disloyal and unseemly man of high office who had so ill-treated her. Obviously, he has beaten a hasty retreat into the nether regions to avoid a vengeful confrontation on a more spiritual plane, where the wronged lady's chances were now at least equal to his own.

The well-documented and perpetual search was revisited upon a specific pathway in the area, notably on moonless nights. Immediately prior to and just after her appearance, the rustle of taffeta is heard nearby. Endlessly seeking only the offending shade of her formerly abusive spouse, an unsuspecting person once accosted by this judgmental apparition, was never faced with such an affront again. Partly because he was proved to be a case of mistaken identity but, more likely, because he was never to be seen in the area again so close to this seat of regal authority – not if he could help it.

Also, on Government House grounds, there is a bell that has been known to tinkle in the orchard whenever thieving hands are about to pluck the fruit and spirit it (pardon the expression) away on a dark night!

The Old Hamilton Prison, Parliament Street

Re-recorded by Mac Musson

This old-time house of detention once carried tales of an injustice perpetrated by our judicial system. Some poor soul was hanged, and it seems the judgment was made on grounds shaky enough to leave doubts in some folk's minds.

Months passed until, suddenly, a series of protests were visited upon the late night wardens – a clank, clank against iron bars, the unmistakable sound of a tin cup clamouring for attention for its holder and issuing from an empty cell block. The racket continued for several nights and many were summoned to lend their ears to this strange commotion. Attention attracted, the noise would stop, and in the silence, there followed a sighing sound, like whispered words echoing over and over, which sounded very much like "You should not have done this to mee-ee-e-e!"

This very nearly sent the already nervous judge into cardiac arrest because he had, over the months, nursed his guilt and doubts, losing countless hours of sleep waiting for the condemned prisoner to come back to haunt him as promised – a threat hurled at him from the dock, as the poor unfortunate was borne away to his execution.

Farcical forces at play you say?

Perhaps in this case, since Bermudians, being a unique brand of individuals with not a little mischief in their make-up, never fail to make the most of a handy situation.

Hasbro House, Paget

As described to Mac Musson by Paul Bourque, CA and Jackie Steele

I was settling in to a new country, my company was in a comfortably central location, and I looked forward to a few years of delightful living. Bermuda! Bright sun, turquoise sea, pink sand – add to this, after a good day's work, tennis, golf and an endless variety of terrific water sports. To have been assigned to this Island of extraordinary beauty was almost beyond one's dreams. I could scarcely credit my good fortune, which, however, was to be tempered by an experience totally foreign to my no-nonsense background.

"I was sharing the apartment dwelling with two friends, Anne, and Jackie Steele, whose bedrooms were a floor above in this rambling old homestead.

After one particularly hectic day, I had gone to bed early and lay there quietly strumming on my old guitar. Judging by the rapidly running footsteps overhead, Jackie had been disturbed while attempting to settle down for the night. Thinking my guitar was the culprit, I quickly put it aside and fell into a sound sleep.

"Anne had yet to return home, and, possibly, it was some subconscious expectancy on my part of doors opening and closing that roused me that night, and for a second or two, my head and eyes didn't want to work together. In disbelief I looked about the room and, seeing someone poking through my bookcase, decided at first it must be Anne, but no – hold it! It was a young punk! Maybe 13 or 14 years old with spiky, fair hair, wearing faded dungarees and an old flannel shirt.

"Hey you! What do you think you're doing?"

"Fully alert now, I jumped out of bed to grab the intruder. The hall light illuminated his features and clothing as he turned to look in my direction. As I reached for him, my hands went through thin air – he had disappeared as I looked at him! Frankly puzzled, I doubted my own senses – THIS JUST DIDN'T HAPPEN – so I decided to keep my own counsel for now, who would believe me anyway!

"Two weeks had passed and I sat with Jackie at the Cock and Feather enjoying the relaxing effects of a much deserved 'Happy Hour', when the subject turned to the strange events at our apartment, which as it turned out, Jackie too had experienced but with slightly differing timetables."

The following is Jackie Steele's side of the story:

"The first time I noticed anything unusual was when I decided to have an early night. I said goodnight to Paul and went to my bedroom which was above the living room. I went into a deep sleep, as

I usually did, but awoke suddenly at about II p.m. I looked over towards my walk-in closet and thought I saw someone going through my clothes. As Paul was the only person in the house, I said, 'Paul?'

"He looked around at me, then turned and continued his searching, now going through my books. I put my bed lamp on and rushed over to my closet but there was no-one there.

"I could hear Paul playing his guitar.

"I decided to think no more of it, jumped back into bed and went to sleep again. I did mention it casually to Anne but not to Paul, as I felt silly.

"A few weeks later, Paul and I were having a drink in the Cock and Feather pub and he started asking me questions like; 'How old is the house?', 'Who owns it?', 'Who lived there before us?', and 'Did anybody die there?'

"I said, 'Why are you asking me all these questions?'

" 'Well', he said, 'promise not to laugh, but the other night I woke up and thought I saw a boy going through my books. I leapt out of bed and held out my fist to thump him, then he disappeared into thin air.'

"It was then I told him what had happened to me. He said he heard me leap out of bed and run across the floor but thought his guitar had awakened me and made me mad.

"We laughed about it and said that the house must be haunted.

"My most frightening experience came later.

"I gave up my room to Anne's Mum and Dad who were staying with us. Her younger brother slept in the living room. I moved into the spare room on the ground floor which had no carpets and was very basically furnished.

"One night I woke up again suddenly at some time after midnight. This time, in the red light caused by my clock-radio, I saw the profile of a boy kneeling at my bedside cabinet facing the clock-radio. I rubbed my eyes and looked more closely but it only confirmed what I thought I had seen. I tried to scream but only a gasp passed my lips. This seemed to startle him and he turned his head and looked me straight in the face with his eyes wide open, as if in fear of being caught. He then stood up and started stepping backwards to the door.

"I sat upright and he smiled at me. He had short fair hair, probably blue eyes and was dressed in a checkered shirt and denim dungarees. He was a tall young boy. I thought, 'I've got a burglar in my bedroom' but still a scream would not come. I was staring at him and he just began to fade before my eyes, still smiling at me.

"I tried to switch my bedroom light on, but, in my panic, hit the clock-radio button and the music started blaring out. At this time I heard Edward, Anne's brother, let out a moan in the other room as if stirring in his sleep. He might have heard me gasp in shock or else the radio disturbed him. I leapt out of bed and ran down the corridor to Anne's room. She came back to the spare room with me – the light was on, the radio still blaring and the sheets thrown back, but nothing else unusual.

"I was too frightened to go back in there and slept with Anne for the rest of the night."
Paul again:

"Some months later the house was being readied for new owners and the contents were up for sale. Jackie was in England, but Anne and I were on hand for the final clearing out of the closet under the staircase, the contents of which were unknown to us until then.

"Amongst all the bits and pieces that had been stored there gathering dust were a quantity of old tintypes and one or two portraits . . . some ornately framed, some just packed in old newspapers to keep the bugs out. They were of only passing interest until, wait . . . 'Turn that one face up again! . . . Anne, look at him will you? It's him! The one in my room that night!' Suffice to say we couldn't leave it at that. The family being at hand, I lost no time in making as near a casual inquiry as possible. How casual can one profess to be when they know they're looking at an exact photo image of the first ghost in one's life? Craftily, I managed to have the portrait set aside to leave in the living room for Jackie to see when she returned the next day – frankly, I was curious to hear her reaction, if any, and so was Anne, who had never experienced anything at all."
Jackie Steele:

"I went to England for two weeks holiday and came back one weekend. The house was empty and the sun shining so I ran upstairs, threw my case down and jumped into my shorts and tee shirt. I then ran down to the living room and, upon entering, froze. Propped up against the sofa was an old and faded portrait of HIM! . . . it was almost life size, 2 to 3 feet high, dingy with age. He was dressed in a soldier's uniform, was holding a rifle with bayonet resting in his hand, the barrel jauntily leaning against his shoulder. He was standing outside a tent. I went hot and then cold and whispered, 'Oh, my God!' before sitting down in a state of shock.

"It was him alright – the piercing eyes and fair complexion. Coming to my senses, I decided I would probably find out that this man still lived on the Island, was about 70 by now but – what sense would that make of my previous experience anyway?

"Paul came home and said, 'What did you think of the picture . . . it was him wasn't it!'

"I agreed.

"The Harriets, owners of the house who now lived in Florida, came around one day when I wasn't in and Anne took the opportunity to ask Mr. Harriet whose portrait it was and what had happened to him.

"Mr. Harriet replied that it was his Uncle Richard, full name – Nathaniel Richard Harriet. He had run away from Bermuda during the First World War and lied about his age in order to fight. He was 16 years old and had been blown apart by shrapnel. He was now buried at Cambridge in England.

"One night, while Anne was away and Paul was out, I felt really creepy on my own, so I sat up in the kitchen and waited for Paul to come home. When he did, we sat and talked about ghosts and hauntings and what we had seen. I told him that I either had to believe in ghosts or that I was going mad. I said I wished 'he' would appear just one more time and then I could be absolutely sure and I would stay calm and try to talk to him. Well, he did appear again. It was shortly after our talk.

"I was lying in bed in my own bedroom and, as usual, in a deep sleep. The rattling of the door-knob woke me. This was the first time 'he' alerted me to his presence by making any kind of sound. I looked over to the door and saw something blurred and fuzzy in front of it. I kept still and just watched as it slowly became the outline of a young boy dressed in what looked like a velvet or corduroy knicker-bocker outfit with a jacket and trousers to the knees. He was running towards me in slow motion but his head was turned, looking behind him as if in alarm. I could only feel compassion for him as he seemed to run from something or someone he feared. In silence, he kept running towards me, fading a couple of feet from my bed. Now I was convinced that his apparition existed.

"Something else I never mentioned before to Paul, is that after I left Bermuda I went to Cambridge to look for 'his' grave. I also looked through a book at a large military cemetery which listed all the names of the war dead and where they were interred. There was no name of Richard Harriet to be found – could his family have been mistaken?"

Footnote: The name given in the above story is an old Bermuda name and would not have been spelled the way our correspondent has it written – it would be Harriott and therefore possibly overlooked in the war memorial ledgers that she perused.

Rendezvous

As told to Joan Skinner by Colin Selley

I t's hard to believe, when you see Bermuda today, that, on this small Island, many Bermudians had summer homes in different locations on the Island. This particular vignette concerns the Selley family, whose homestead was in Pembroke, on Pitt's Bay Road, but whose summer residence was a cottage called Rendezvous overlooking Grape Bay in Paget.

The Selley family would close up their Pitt's Bay house in June, and move, with furniture, food, clothing – all this without benefit of motorized transportation! – to take up residence on the South Shore for the summer. Colin's father, Roy Selley, later to become Mayor of the City of Hamilton, would work in town during the week, and arrive in Paget for the weekend.

This particular year, 1944, the ninth annual migration had taken place without incident, and all were settled in to enjoy the summer on Grape Bay.

Rap, rap, rap! Thump, thump, thump! What WAS going on? This was not "things that go bump in the night!", it was a case of BUMPS in the night! The noise so loud that some nights the family would sleep at a neighbour's house. Not exactly a terrifying experience, but certainly an audio one. To go to sleep to the gentle lapping of surf on sand, only to awaken to what sounded for all the world like the percussion section of the Royal Philharmonic in the last throes of the 1812 Overture!

"We had all the wiring checked and the floorboards pulled up – even the pipes were pulled out of the walls – but we didn't drive him away!" laughed Colin.

Soon friends were rallying round trying to find the source of the rapping and thumping. Some stationed themselves in the basement, others upstairs in the living room. Those in the basement would swear the noise was coming from upstairs, while those in the living room stated that absolutely, positively, the noise was coming from the basement! When the rapping began, there would be much confusion as those in the basement rushed upstairs only to be met on the narrow stairway by the living room contingent rushing down!

The news of these goings-on travelled swiftly having been covered extensively by The Royal Gazette, and soon families were bringing picnic suppers to the area, spending the evening listening to the sounds otherworldly, and watching the human confusion.

This poltergeistic activity invaded the cottage at lonely Grape Bay that summer of 1944, and, strangely, was never in evidence again.

Inland in Pembroke 1966

An experience recorded by cousins, Richard and Paul Card to Mac Musson

Inland is a house of modest age and without energy forms of its own, but for two weeks it acted as a holding station for anguished manifestations seemingly in search of my daughter and myself, their lost friends.

We weren't in residence for very long when my father called to say we were to spend Christmas with the family in Florida and to make the necessary arrangements. We had Teddy, the cat, and the two dogs – good old George and young, God forgive us the name, Angusina, a terrified Labrador who never did overcome her wall-eyed reaction to strange encounters. Angusina was always hiding behind something and never did get the hang of being blasé like George.

Moving household is a tedious chore so we were pleased to be able to anticipate a change of scene in which we could relax over the holidays. To this end, we turned to friends who were about to become very "tried and true" indeed, to house and dog – sit for us while we were gone.

The following is Paul's account:

"Drawers were opened, doors left ajar, things went missing and, for a surprise effect, items fell out of cupboards even though the doors had been closed! And, repeatedly, on the stairs and down the hallway – footsteps, agitated footsteps. Add to this the overwhelming sense of someone standing at the bathroom door as you bathed – someone who didn't answer when you called out and wasn't there when, dripping wet, you unlocked the door to look."

Richard Card says: "Then the electric organ playing downstairs with no one there. At first I thought it was Paul fooling around but he was late home that night, the doors and windows were all locked and, as it turned out when I got downstairs, the damned thing wasn't even switched on!

"At the kitchen window . . . a flame burst into being like a muffled firework! The whole area outside the sill was awash with flickering blue light, and, as suddenly, was gone. After inspecting the outside and finding no trace of spent fireplay, I resignedly returned to the kitchen and decided to call it a night.

"This nonsense continued for ten days, subsiding just before the family returned from the States.

"If 'someone' was looking for Mussons, it sure as hell missed them!"

Edelweiss, Pitt's Bay, Pembroke

Two tales reported by Pat Butterfield to Mac Musson

This is the home of Pat and Than Butterfield, which briefly developed a presence that seemed to manifest an aura of resistance – because of a young woman who house-sat for a few weeks.

Strangely, she was not allowed upstairs to the bedrooms, she felt held back at the foot of the stairs.

She wound up "camping" on the couch in the living room.

It is thought that it could only be a prim and proper old Mrs. Butterfield who continued watching out for the proprieties.

The young lady and her male companion weren't married you see.

Watlington & Conyers

These offices on Front Street, Hamilton once housed Godet and Young's business and it is there the shade of Dolly Joell makes regular visits, obviously searching for someone or something. Pat Butterfield saw her early one morning. Stories have it that Dolly Joell wore white, and true to form, she was in a white dress and wore a shawl. Pat waited for her to speak wondering at her old fashioned attire, and suddenly realized she was gone . . . poof!

Like Pat, many have met her face to face and suffer no ill effects other than a slight shock the first time around. Dolly Joell was an employee of long-standing and was a familiar figure to all her friends and customers as she walked to and from Collector's Hill to work every day.

Pat Butterfield's husband, Than, when approached on the subject said, "Oh yes, Dolly's an occasional visitor. I didn't tell you about her because I didn't want to alarm you."

Pat's dry "Thanks a lot!" went unnoticed.

Gibbs Hill Lighthouse

117 feet high and 185 spiralling steps to the viewing platform and lightwell
Told to Mac Musson by Michael Dolding

Completed and activated on May 1, 1846, accounts of unaccountable events at Gibbs Hill Lighthouse have been noted by a few past lighthouse keepers. The following was related to Mac Musson by Michael Dolding of Marine & Ports, part of whose job it is to oversee the care of our two lighthouses! Since reports along the same lines are heard from other folk, one wonders at the strange recording of someone's anxiety from the past that left this on-going impression for others to hear.

Said Mike Dolding:

"We lived in Gibbs Hill's Lighthouse cottage during this period and, as is often the case as a built-in watchkeeper, I was, on occasion, required to make a breathless dash to the top when the lighthouse machinery failed to operate fully. All this means is that when the light comes on it remains steady without rotating, which, in itself, usually requires little more than whoever is on hand to get up there and give it the necessary shove that sets things in motion once again.

"On this particular evening, as soon as it was clear that a nudge was needed, I made the usual call to Bill Montgomery, the attendant electrician, in case the problem turned out to be more serious, and then proceeded to the light chamber 185 steps above. On this occasion I took Beans, my feisty little terrier, as company, giving him his evening's exercise at the same time. He loved zipping up the stairs, always getting to the top long before me. Of course, I knew I'd have to carry him on the return 'flight' downwards . . . he often ran out of steam at that point!

"On this night I eventually caught up with him in the lighthouse well and found that it was indeed straightforward . . . a little coaxing from the sidelines had the machinery locking into its nightly merry-go-round . . . and a wasted trip for old Bill was on the cards but, as always, once he was there it was advisable to have him double check the intricacies of this finely balanced apparatus.

"I stood by to wait, enjoying the spectacle of the Bermuda islands at nightfall, the sinking trails of sunset, the blues of outer space, the ebony cast of the land and coast and the lights . . . the living sparkle of street and homelights putting the stars to shame for the moment. Always one is held spellbound by such visual splendour so at variance with its daytime vividness. All spells are made to be broken however, and, after calling Harbour Radio to report all well, I was readying for the downward haul with pup in arms. Turning, I heard quite distinctly the sound of footsteps hurrying up the stairs . . . 'Great, I thought, here comes old Bill' . . . the terrier ran to the top of the stairs as if to add his welcome, only to come to an abrupt halt, stiffen, and then, with his hackles standing on end, began alternately to whine, snarl and bark. Now then, I thought, this is not on. What the hell is wrong with the silly dog! . . .

"Darkness hadn't fully settled in and from the catwalk I could just make out the ground below. Silly, I had thought I'd locked the entrance door after I came in but must've been mistaken. Yet, I couldn't make out anything below that looked like Bill's car. Funny . . . the dog was shivering and resumed his frantic behaviour, this time keeping it up. My insides began to quake and I went cold all over. What is this? My own hair is standing on end now. More footsteps! . . . going down this time? For the first time in my life I knew what it was like to nearly suffocate on the heartbeat in my throat. God, if it wasn't Bill, what was it!

"After about ten minutes that seemed an eternity the dog quietened and looked down the stairs, tail now awag. Wait for no more Mike Dolding! . . . I grabbed the dog and ran down as fast as I could, checking landings as I went . . . nothing! At the entrance door all was still and in semi-darkness. The door was securely locked after all! I let myself out, locking up as I went, and putting the dog down in time to see him take off in happy welcome, Bill had just arrived and was getting out of his car.

"He took the key and went to check things out. I said nothing and, I might add, I never went up there again at night without some company – usually my wife, my dog AND a rum and ginger!

"I have often wondered if perhaps the presence or ghost of one of the early lighthouse keepers prowls the beacon at night, checking that all is well and the light is on and operating correctly. I had been utterly spooked and still shudder at the memory."

This sketch is adapted from the mural by Sheilagh Head in the coffee shop of the King Edward VII Memorial Hospital.

The Old Rectory, St. George's

Re-recorded by Mac Musson

Now a Bermuda National Trust property, the Old Rectory is open to the public once a week. Once each month, in the early hours of the morning, the sound of an ethereal spinet echoes daintily through the old house. As one tenant described it –

"Like the tinkling of bells – gentle, happy tunes."

The Rectory for St. Peter's Church was built in 1705 and it is likely that a spinet or harpsichord, popular at that time, would have been part of its early furnishings.

Mrs. Charles (Jeanette) Outerbridge resided there for many years and once enjoyed this charming visitation, never feeling anything but a fond kinship with whoever it was at the old-time keyboard of a long gone musical instrument.

The Cathedral of The Most Holy Trinity, Hamilton

Recorded by Mac Musson

Our visitors are not exempt from the past. We can tell you of two incidences, totally unrelated, and involving people from different walks of life and very different locations on the North American continent.

One involves a couple of middle age who were fascinated with the structure and background of the Hamilton Cathedral of the Most Holy Trinity. Having spent considerable time studying the interior, the husband went to stroll around the grounds while his wife completed her examination of the Raredos behind the altar. The cathedral was cool and a pleasant relief and she was in no hurry to return to the heat and humidity that awaited her outside. Eventually she could put it off no longer, and stepped out into the brilliant sunshine, adjusting her eyes to the glare. She then spotted her husband standing down by the restored section of the exterior, deeply engaged in what looked to be an earnest conversation with the wall.

Not sure of how to handle this, she slowly made her way towards her absorbed spouse – clearly he was having some kind of overcoming and, to make matters worse, wasn't wearing his cap.

Reaching his side, she tentatively tapped him on the shoulder – "Bill – it's time we went, come along."

Bill turned with a cheerful grin saying "Hi, Hon, come join us, this gentleman is telling me about the fire they had, and is working on the restoration. The way they get the stone is really interesting . . . ." Seeing the look on his wife's face, he looked back to his erstwhile companion, only to find he and his tools of the trade had disappeared.

To him the experience had been real – to his concerned wife, it was time he got out of the sun.

Bridge House, St. George's

As told to Mac Musson by Jill Raine

This distraught woman, a visitor not wishing to identify herself, called artist Jill Raine, who manages Bridge House, to ask her if she knew its history, and if so, if it contained any details that might account for her dreadful experience as she crossed the bridged entrance from the street.

She went on to explain that she had resisted the idea of coming to Bermuda for many years even though the opportunities had been many. She'd had no idea why this dread persisted, since she had never been here and was only here now due to her husband's insistence. He was attending his company's convention at the Southampton Princess and since wives had been included, he wanted her with him.

After settling in, her friends had insisted she go with them to St. George's on a bus tour, a standard part of the sightseeing programmes serving groups staying in our hotels.

Once there, she began coming to terms with her fears and was beginning to enjoy herself.

Inevitably, they came to Bridge House, an old landmark with its own rocking chair ghost, as well as a present day art gallery and gift shop. Once inside this charming setting, with all its art works, crafts and mementoes of Bermudiana, she suddenly was overwhelmed by a most terrible fear accompanied by an unaccountable sense of hysteria. She simply had to get out! Visibly disturbed, tearful and shaking, she was quickly helped from the doorway and back to the street where someone ran into the nearby pub for water or brandy or both!

Needless to say her tour lost its charm and she went back to the hotel, retiring to her room in an effort to rid herself of this unaccountable depression. She'd never felt like that before and NEVER lost control of her emotions in a public environment. Shuddering at the memory, she spent a restless night determining to make the aforesaid enquiries about the old walkway the following morning. Jill was unable to help her, but suggested she contact some local historians, giving her one or two references. The mystified lady failed to follow up however, as no one heard from her, and we are sure she left the island for the first and last time.

Jill Raine knew of my interest and involvement with haunted environs and told me about the odd occurrence, asking me what I made of it, if anything. At the time I was as puzzled as anyone else, but more recently have completed a small article on Bermuda's past bout with witchcraft for a travel book on Bermuda.

As chronicler of this tale, I can only offer the following, inconclusive as it may be, but, it is at least interesting to note:

On May 20th, 1653, Mistress Christian Stevenson, having been tried and sentenced to hang, was duly escorted to Hangman's Island, across from the square in St. George's.

At that time the creek still ran through the town square past where Bridge House now stands, emptying into the waterway that runs between the Town Square and Ordnance Island. Of course, there was a wooden foot-bridge over the narrow width of the creek for pedestrian use, and it was at this point, later, in the 1690s, that Bridge House came into being.

The distraught and stunned victims of these tragic persecutions, were, each in their turn, conveyed from their place of confinement, across the foot-bridge, and past this point under guard, as they made their way to the gallows. History notes that this poor unfortunate woman attempted to break free of her captors, weeping and crying out her innocence to anyone in the gathering crowd who might offer her help. Since a sympathizer might be looked upon as a dabbler in the Black Arts himself, no one came forward to help, and her vain attempt to break free was quickly aborted. She was returned to custody, in all probability, very nearly on the same spot where this present day visitor suffered from this disturbingly realistic, yet blighted "recall".

Was this incident to suggest temporary 'possession' by a traumatized entity, or could it have been a form of spontaneous regression? Who can say.

"There are more things in Heaven and Earth, Horatio!" quoth the Bard.

Post Script: The building of Bridge House was begun in 1690, and in 1696, the trial of Sarah Spencer, the last woman to be accused of witchcraft, took place. She was not found guilty, as far as we know, since there is no record to be found to that effect. The trauma of her experience, however, may well have left a stigma on the surrounds whilst her fate hung in the balance and her fellowmen and women stood by to watch, briefly indulging in the unseemly thrill of another's unwarranted misfortune. Their relief at her release could not have been as great as her own but the shame they may well have felt would have served well in preventing anything of this kind happening again. Nor did it.

Loyal Hill, Smith's

"where sounds of silence now abound."
by Mac Musson

When an old house is extensively renovated, many of the historical origins may suffer permanent disorientation. Add to this bulldozers on the surrounding land, flattening and leaving nothing visible behind, and, maybe, even laying low a few ghostly intruders whose presence might have been suspected in the past. Bulldozers definitely take the magic out of things.

The matriarch of the old Scott Gilbert family had a great belief in the "little people" and supernatural surrounds, and the young of the family were accustomed to considerations being given in this direction. The homestead was a warm and friendly one, and so it was not unnatural to hear singing and laughter emanating from its interior, influencing the atmosphere while mystifying neighbours who began to realize that some of the most charming and melodious sounds issued from the house when nobody was home.

Mrs. Cyril Smith, formerly Dora Gilbert, spent her girlhood in company with these unseen guests, suffering not at all from the effects. Noises of activities galore would be heard on occasion and pictures were always being knocked off walls while objects were moved from their normal places when the family was away. It was taken in stride, and the melodies wafting on the air taken as a gift of the moment to be sorely missed when they ceased, as, of course, they eventually did in the face of advancing multi-dwelling developments. Today, even Loyal Hill is no longer identifiable as the old manor house it used to be, and the hillside no longer has a mystical quality. The old family matriarch would be saddened at the loss, for what is lovelier than fancied fairies, and good angels keeping a protective watch over you as you played and slept. This was Dora's belief and, in a way, could only have served as a delightful legacy to hand down to her children's children.

Brimstone Hill House

As told to Mac Musson by Babs Abbott McKenna and Terri Drew

Historically the house dates back to the late 1700s when yet another sea captain made ready to create his home. Often this was done with the spoils from distant ports which were used to either construct their houses or furnish their lusty interiors. Captain Jack Smith made his mark on Bermuda but not an entirely pleasant one on his crew. At least it is fairly certain from what quarter came the assailant who struck him dead outside his back door and stole the sock Captain Jackie had filled with money, preparing to secret it away in some unknown corner of his house.

Brimstone Hill was designed to emulate a ship's superstructure, bridge and wheelhouse with port and starboard lookout wings as quarters . . . an old seadog's idea of how a landlubber's dwelling should be laid out. Captain Smith had a jealous regard for his home and viewed it with great pride.

Today Brimstone Hill is the home of Terri and Michael Drew and was formerly the family home of Terri's parents, Pete and artist, Babs Abbott. Pete was a well-respected architect in Bermuda and in 1951 had made the decision to renovate the old house, which is situated on the South Shore in Devonshire. By 1952 the rather extensive renovations were nearly completed; the original design had undergone considerable architectural changes . . . for the better it was thought at the time.

Feeling restless on this particular evening as renovations neared completion, Pete was making the rounds of the house. Quite unexpectedly, he beheld the figure of a weathered old seaman standing in the corner of the living room, wearing a reefer and woollen cap.

Preoccupied, Pete's momentum had carried him into the next room, before mentally registering what he thought he had seen, and doing an unscheduled turn-about for the proverbial double-take. The indignant old salt was still there! About to speak, Pete's scalp prickled as his eyes locked with the angry glare of this vaporous image for the second time within minutes, before it slowly dissipated into nothing. Bemused, he retired to his bedroom to take stock of his powers of observation. Had he, or hadn't he just seen something out of the ordinary and if so, why was this happening to him?

And where on earth was the dog? It wasn't like Mugsy to ignore his master's voice.

Calling repeatedly, Pete made his way back past the living room to seek out his unresponsive hound, applying the old ostrich's head-in-the-sand routine as he went, in the hope that, if he didn't look, surely 'it' would go away!

Pete got to the front door and, several yards away, sat Mugsy, firmly ensconced in the middle of the moonlit lawn, refusing to budge! The customary delights to be found in the homestead held no attraction for him whatsoever. Loyalty had taken a back seat, for Mugsy clearly was not about to answer Pete's summonses. "Humph – stay there then," muttered Pete to himself, and went indoors.

Gradually, Pete felt the house settle down and the sense of a 'presence' departed. Only now did Mugsy, with a casual yawn, rise from his self-imposed exile and return to the house, curling up on his favourite mat and glancing disdainfully at Pete as if nothing untoward had happened.

Old Captain Jackie may not have been taking these changes to his old home lightly; the "appearance" certainly suggested the presence of a strong personality standing by. There have been reports of homes, in other parts of the world, that seem to resist change but, to be fair, some apparitions have also been known to appear in an attempt to prevent accidents. If this was the reason for the two sightings, the warning didn't have the desired effect, for, as the Abbotts' were happily getting on with settling in, the modernized pumproom blew up. A monumental set-back.

What caused the explosion that was heard for miles around during the dawn hours that shook the new section to its very foundations was at first uncertain, but, the newly installed boiler bore no resemblance to its former self and, Captain Jackie was never seen again!

Cautious examination after the event was not conclusive and no one was hurt. The tantrum, if that's what it was, had spent itself in one enormous blast. In the realm of 'ifs', it was certainly one way to have the last word!

Winterhaven in Smith's Parish

As recorded in an interview with 'Heidi' by Joan Skinner

Winterhaven, its brooding façade facing the sea, sits imposingly on the South Shore in Smith's Parish. Originally it was privately owned, and for many years remained boarded up while children and would-be vandals gave it a wide berth. It was finally purchased by the Bermuda Government about 10 years ago and is now rented, and this tale concerns two young ladies who were house-sitting while the tenants were off the Island.

This is a taped interview with a very attractive European-born resident of Bermuda who wishes that her name not be used, so in keeping with her origins, we're going to call her 'Heidi'. Because her choice of phrasing is so delightful, we're going to keep it exactly the way she said it.

Joan: "How did you get to Winterhaven?"

"A friend, Irene, and I were asked to baby-sit Winterhaven and I accepted, although I heard that it was haunted, but, of course, you don't believe it until you have your own experiences. I remember the first thing that happened. Irene was in the shower and I heard a whistling. I asked her if she was whistling but she called back, "No." It was a melody, and it was all around.

"I said, 'That's funny; who is playing a trick here!'

"Irene could hear it when she got out of the shower and she went out to check – but the whistling stopped.

"The next thing was, we were going upstairs to bed, and the doors didn't really lock, although I always felt I should lock myself in. Suddenly, it was very clear, somebody was walking up the steps. We dashed out the door and I was very brave, standing behind Irene, and nobody. Absolutely nobody.

"We went to bed and, suddenly, I woke up. I felt very cold and didn't know why. I was lying on my side in bed and suddenly saw something misty in the corner of the bedroom. It almost took on a shape, but I couldn't make it out but there was something there that shouldn't be there. Suddenly this mist started to move towards me. It just came closer, and I thought, 'I'm not experiencing this; my eyes are playing tricks on me.'

"Suddenly it was standing in front of me, this misty thing. I could now even make out the arms and I thought to myself, I remember this so clearly, 'If I look up and make out a face, I'm going to scream!' I closed my eyes and lay completely still hardly even to breathe. I don't know how long, every moment seemed endless but, when I opened my eyes – clear! It was completely gone.

"We often heard many unusual and unexplainable noises. One night I woke up and heard, I know this sounds crazy, it was noises on top of the roof. It was as if somebody was moving furniture, pushing the heavy stuff. But somebody else heard it as well! We had a houseguest, and the next morning he said he had woken up, he didn't know what time it was, and he said he heard noises like somebody moving furniture. I felt this was confirmation of what I had heard."

The wife of another former tenant, known to Heidi, demonstrated some truly bizarre changes of character while in the house, and had said to Heidi on several occasions, 'They're on the roof, they're on the roof.' And, as Heidi said:

"So when I myself heard the noises on the roof, it didn't really surprise me all that much as also I realized that my poor friend had been misjudged. That house seemed to change people, especially women!

"It was the last day and I was cleaning the house. I always get panicky about losing my keys, so I put them carefully on the bedside table while I cleaned the master bedroom and bath. I was starting to scrub the bathroom when I heard this incredible noise. I get goosebumps just thinking about it! AND SHE DID!

"I thought it had sounded like somebody had thrown my keys on the floor. I dashed out but there was no one in the bedroom, and I checked downstairs – but nobody. I came back up and suddenly I noticed that my keys weren't anymore on the night table. I thought I was crazy! Suddenly my brain was functioning again and THERE were my keys, about five feet away from the table on the wooden floor. And when I went to pick up the keys, I felt freezing cold. I was so cold, yet it was a lovely sunny day and I was perspiring from scrubbing the tub. How could this be?

"The most amazing thing happened when I had packed up and was going back to my own cottage. I went to open my front door and my master key was bent by about 15 degrees. Now, this is a master key and that key to bend is impossible! It was like whatever was at Winterhaven wanted me to stay . . . I wasn't going to get in my own house! Also, it was the only key on the ring that was bent."

When the Winterhaven tenants returned, Heidi asked the wife if she had any experiences in the house, and she said she had. The wife knew that there were unexplainable incidents which took place.

She said, "Actually there was a medium visiting from England and she came to the house at our invitation. After a while, the medium felt that there had been a woman who lived in the house who discovered her husband had been a philanderer. The woman committed suicide, after long years in an institution somewhere away, but in life had supposedly vowed that no other woman would be happy in that house."

The wife went on to say that she had had many encounters in the house but her husband thought she was overly imaginative, if not a trifle crazy, and was encouraging her to see a psychiatrist.

"I went to bed one night, and awoke a while later. There was a man standing over me in a period costume. I sat up in bed and screamed and screamed, but when my husband turned on the light it was gone."

Another time the family had gone out, leaving their German Shepherd dog locked in the house. Their windows were also locked and all bedroom doors left firmly closed. When they returned their bedroom doors were still closed and the dog greeted them in the usual manner, but when they opened the door and entered the master bedroom, they found it completely ransacked – bed torn apart, furniture moved and overturned.

There is a radio talk show, Bermuda's Living Memories, hosted by a delightful character stage-named "Blondell" and aired on Sunday mornings. Quite recently, by sheer coincidence, if you still happen to believe in it, one of our merry group of compilers tuned into the programme which happened to be on haunted houses. A chap phoned in to tell his tale of the unexplainable.

It seems that he and three co-workers, old Bermudian masons and truckers, had been hired to clean out Winterhaven prior to its undergoing renovations some years ago. One of the items to be removed and taken to the dump was an old cast-iron wood-burning stove in the old-fashioned kitchen. It was so heavy and awkward that it took the four of them to maneuver it to the kitchen door. Once there, they concluded that they would need another of their mates to get it through the door and out to the truck. This realization and the appointed lunch hour arrived simultaneously and, being hard workers who made an early start, hunger won the day, so they decided to take their break and return afterwards to finish the job.

Once back on the job with all hands ready to work the massive old stove onto its side and out, they found it was no longer where they had left it. It had taken itself back nearly 16 feet, almost to its starting point! The numbers of their crew who would be caught dead in that house after that totaled minus zero.

Local artist, Molly Critchley, recalled visiting a friend who lived there some time before, and after hearing we were including Winterhaven in this book she said, "I'll never forget that occasion! – I sat there in the living room having tea one afternoon and all the time I was trying to talk to my friend, I kept having to push my hair back off my face. Every time I did, it was immediately flipped back again just as if some disagreeably childish person was taunting me. Eventually, in exasperation I muttered, 'Dear me this is so annoying! It's almost as if someone is deliberately mussing my hair into my face!'" . . . .

"Someone is," was my hostess' reply, "things like that go on all the time here. It hates it if you do, but TRY to ignore it."

Casa Rosa

As told to Mac Musson by Diana Diel

Casa Rosa was built around 1855 and for a long time the lower road-side floor housed a small grocery store . . . Sir John Cox could remember getting his candy treats there when he was a youngster, and over the years since, it has served many as hearth and home, not always being treated as well as it might in the past.

Diana Diel: "Repeatedly we tried to remove the old resident cat to less lonely and more amenable surroundings, indeed, when we left Casa Rosa we took him with us to what we felt was a far nicer home with a family prepared to look after him in his dotage. We had grown quite fond of this unaccountably dedicated creature, this old Tom with such endearing friendliness in his character. It didn't seem to matter how far we took him away from his habitat, however, he eventually found his way back to sit it out with any and all manner of passing new tenants, whether they wanted him or not. He seemed to belong there, a perpetual companion to some unseen host. It was much later we learned that he had probably been the devoted companion and pet of the tragic Rebecca."

And who was Rebecca? Imagine for the moment that you knew her, a lady who understood and accepted responsibility for her ailing parent and who remained a spinster, setting aside her personal dreams and ambitions. A selfless woman now long past her prime but upon whom the years still sat so kindly . . . and then there was the gift, and with it her days were made the more bearable as she played and sang for her own pleasure, as well as her father and friends.

What must it be like to have a singing voice of exceptional quality and yearn to give pleasure to the listeners of the world and find yourself bogged down with a filial duty so overwhelming there is no hope but to attend to the need oneself. So it was with Rebecca . . . .

There can be little doubt that, of the many who knew her, there were those who silently rejoiced at her release when, at last, her ailing father passed to his reward. Now she was free to pursue her heart's desire. And Rebecca hesitated only briefly. Encouraged by those who knew her talent, Rebecca set forth for the mainland to follow her starcrossed path. Her voice must surely grow under a teacher's command. This was to be her one positive attempt to grasp what had almost become for her, an impossible dream.

As she began her studies, her health failed. Illness threatened to end her life. This splendid voice made to sing was destined to be stilled. What great penance was this? Ill and defeated, her time running out, she returned to her Island home. A tabby kitten awaited her, a gift from a sympathetic neighbour for comfort and companionship, his smallness and affection a warm distraction.

Diana Diel recalls the one singularly funny day when a pleasant looking lady passed by her kitchen door as she spoke on the phone. Simultaneously she heard her mother greet this same person through the side window and then come up as if to receive her when she reached the entrance to the upper living room where her sister, Sheelagh, was reading a book. Having both been impressed with the "sighting," they reached the parlour door together, EXCEPT for the visitor they went to meet. Quite impossibly "she" had completely disappeared leaving the two women of the house looking askance at one another while the old grey cat sat calmly on the doorsill looking intently down the stairs – and purring.

"Previously there had been those who claimed they had seen an ethereal lady going the rounds indoors and on the outside steps leading to the living room above, but we weren't aware of this at the time.

"Then there was the matter of a piano playing some wistful melody from time to time. When it was casually mentioned to some friends, it was said without so much as a smile, 'Oh, that's Rebecca. She often played the piano for people who stayed there. Don't let it upset you, she's harmless.'

"At first we thought it was the old cat walking tunefully across the keys, but on several occasions my mother made certain, before going to bed, that the lid was down over the keys and STILL the sound of musical notes was heard!!!"

Diana and her sister frequently and bemusedly recall the strangeness of Casa Rosa and the unusual behaviour of the old grey cat who, it is said, attained a great age before finally passing into Rebecca's waiting world – oddly enough, it was after he let go of life that Rebecca did, in fact, seem to cease her lonely wanderings around the old homestead.

More recent tenants and owners were mostly concerned with the removal of the old piano which had reached the point of no return, costing more to repair, than to buy new. The disastrous old Steinway, circa 1904, was a shadow of its former days of grandeur – "not a tinkle left in it."

Hughie and Penny Watlington have been told of many occasions in the past where bottles rattled in their place on top of the antique armoire as its doors kept opening and closing on their own. Remaining for them however, is the regular occurence of the backdoor opening, followed by soft footsteps – always across the upstairs hall and down the back stairs.

Newly renovated and restored by the Watlingtons, Casa Rosa has had its old world charm enhanced, and the downstairs rooms seem to be alive with atmosphere.

Warm and reassuring, they almost – purr.

P.S. Both Diana Diel and her mother were pianists. Sister Sheelagh was not, and Diana wonders if this sympathetic sharing of interests, was what enabled the two of them to make a brief contact with this remnant of Rebecca's gentle spirit.

Dean Hall in Flatts

As reported to Joan Skinner by Peter Outerbridge

Clustered in and around Flatts Village are many homes with strange stories attached to them. History abounds and theatrical replays occur from time to time. From the Aquarium, past Lazy Corner, up through the hillside and beyond, one pursues these sensitive tales.

This story concerns a moment in time at Dean Hall on Flatts Hill. For those to whom it happened, there is no turning aside the impact of dual observation, triple if you count the old dog, that briefly loomed out of the past.

It was about 1953. The setting, the old study cum-music room at Dean Hall nestled atop Flatts Hill near the magnificent expanse of Harrington Sound. Here we have the grand piano to one side near the stairwell, and, to the right, the over-stuffed couch above which hangs a large portrait of Peter's old-time neighbour, Jimmy Outerbridge, who died in the Second World War. His portrait was done in happier times before Hitler turned the world upside-down.

Curled up in a corner was the family dog, who had been the devoted companion of the man in the portrait, deceased these past few years. He was a large, respectably antique, and extremely laid-back Dalmatian.

Looking at the portrait, Peter couldn't help recall childhood memories; going fishing with his younger brother, John, at Flatts Inlet and, in passing, hearing Jimmy Outerbridge striving through yet another piano lesson. The periodic rap of a ruler across his knuckles for mistakes, beating a disgruntled tattoo against the steadier insistence of the metronome, while his dog, then young and boisterous, sat panting impatiently, yearning, with his young master, for freedom from the tedious weight of scales and arpeggios imposed upon them.

Peter, naturally, rejoiced in his own freedom. Sunny Saturdays were meant for fishing only! Fate, however, frequently gives life a little twist.

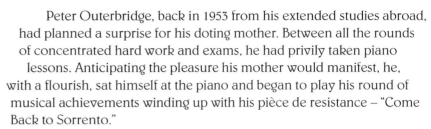

Peter Outerbridge, back in 1953 from his extended studies abroad, had planned a surprise for his doting mother. Between all the rounds of concentrated hard work and exams, he had privily taken piano lessons. Anticipating the pleasure his mother would manifest, he, with a flourish, sat himself at the piano and began to play his round of musical achievements winding up with his pièce de resistance – "Come Back to Sorrento."

The poignant strains of Sorrento approached its closing bars with its accompanying crescendo, Peter's mother sat listening, enthralled. The old dog suddenly rose to his feet, padded to the couch, and climbed up to place his large paws on the backrest beneath the portrait – tail awag. As the dog gazed in rapt attention, Peter and his mother held themselves in stunned silence. Jimmy Outerbridge's smiling portrait acquired a third dimension, literally stepping out into the room as if to touch the waiting dog beneath it!

Neither spoke at first, then as they looked askance at one another beginning to utter the question they recognized looming in one another's eyes, both turned tail and ran from the room.

Italy was where Jimmy died, shot by a German guard as he tried to escape from a moving train.

In later years, both Peter and his mother acknowledged a sincere regret that they hadn't the presence of mind to accept what they saw as a special privilege given at a moment of unconscious oneness. Fear, although purely reactionary, had uprooted them, when love would have calmed them into receiving this gift of insight!

Verdmont

by John Cox

A large number of Bermuda's eighteenth century homes are said to be haunted, perhaps none more than the Bermuda National Trust's historic Verdmont Museum in Smith's Parish.

Verdmont is an impeccable example of local early Georgian architecture. Built around 1710 in the style of the small English manor house, it is four squared with four great chimneys, two at each end, which provide for a fireplace in each of the eight rooms.

In the summer of 1951, Verdmont was purchased from the Joell family by the Bermuda Historical Monuments Trust, predecessor of the Bermuda National Trust, who restored it as the pride of the Trust's house museums.

I joined the staff in January 1982 and still enjoy working at Verdmont one day a week.

Sometimes, standing at the staircase with my hand on the beautifully turned handrail in the immense peace of this fine old house, I feel certain NOW will be the time I see a ghost, but all that greets me is the tapping of the cherry branches on the windowpane and the quiet rustling of palmettos in the garden. There are those at Verdmont however, who have had real encounters with the supernatural.

One sultry afternoon back in August of 1982, I was showing a lone woman around the house and was soon aware that she was becoming increasingly disturbed by something in the house. Upstairs, in the main bedroom, she told me she felt the presence of the spirit of a teenage girl. The spirit was unhappy and wandered aimlessly about the room. I wondered whether this was the ghost of John Trott's only daughter who died of typhoid in that very room as long ago as 1844.

As with all of my visitors, I invited the woman to see the attic while I descended the stairs to the drawing room. Minutes later I heard a gasping sound from upstairs; then quick footsteps on the staircase. In the next instant the woman appeared before me, pale and breathless.

"You have a ghost in the attic," she stammered. "I saw a man up there. He appeared to me in the corner of the room, then just faded away." The woman was visibly shaken and left the house immediately.

Later that year, when one of the attendants was closing the upstairs shutters at the end of the day, she turned around to see a woman in eighteenth century costume, arms folded and staring at her as if puzzled. Then the woman turned and walked away, down the corridor and into the Oriental Room. The attendant followed, only to find that no one was there. Yet she knew positively that the mysterious woman HAD walked into that room.

Suddenly she felt cold all over; she had encountered a ghost.

The first curator, the late Mrs. Lillian Fox, would frequently hear strange sounds emanating from the attic.

"It was like a rope, coiled several times over, being thrown on the floor. Rope is not kept in the attic and we never could find any logical reasons for the sounds," explained Mrs. Fox.

Then late one winter afternoon in 1980, Mrs. Fox was doing some light cleaning in the attic and the figure of a man appeared by her side.

"It was getting dark, and the figure was not well defined, more fuzzy than anything, but it was definitely a man and I feel sure it was Mr. Spencer Joell who lived at 'Verdmont' up until the 1940s. I had known Mr. Joell personally. He was always a good friend to me," said Mrs. Fox.

Perhaps the strangest tale of all is that related by a New Jersey couple who visited the house back in 1976. The couple was fascinated by the attic and took several photographs of it and its furnishings which include a Victorian doll's house. When they returned home and had the films developed, one revealed the outline of a tall, thin man seated next to the doll's house. The photo was sent to Mrs. Fox who thought that the mysterious figure bore a distinct resemblance to Mr. Joell.

"Poor Spencer Joell, he spent the last years of this life in a nursing home and hated being torn away from Verdmont. I believe that the spirits here died under unhappy circumstances so they are not at peace and wander about confused, as though they are in limbo," concluded Mrs. Fox.

Lillian Fox died in December 1983. Since her death there have been no sightings of ghosts at Verdmont, but there are times when Verdmont's atmosphere becomes so alive with the past, it is not hard to imagine the gentlemen of yesteryear, bewigged in their knee-britches, shoe-buckles and silver-hilted swords; their ladies tight-laced and flounced, going about their daily duties in the old house.

As you leave Verdmont in the quickly gathering twilight, you may stop and glance back in awe at the shuttered house whose memories live and sleep somewhere between its ancient walls.

From a recently turned up account from an old Bermuda News Bureau release: Miss Lilian Joell, daughter of Spencer Joell, once confided to a friend, a Miss Helen Durrieux, that during her many years at Verdmont, she would often be aware of the rustling of long taffeta skirts on the stairs and voices whispering "Be quiet or she'll hear us." While these periodic visitations took place, her dog performed in a manner unlike his normal self. It's not that he went berserk, but he was decidedly disconcerted, demonstrating his total displeasure at finding something "there" he couldn't really get his teeth into. Verdmont is open to the public daily except Sundays. There is a small admission fee.

Spithead
by John Cox

Standing like a monument to its builder, Hezekiah Frith, Spithead, above Turtle Bay in Warwick, evokes a past rich with history. Captain Frith (1763-1848) has gone down in Bermuda history as the Island's foremost skipper and privateer. At the age of 22 he obtained Letters of Marque from the King, and became so prosperous in the capture of French and Spanish merchant ships that he was able to buy several large tracts of land in Warwick. On the northernmost extremity of his property, on a point of land jutting out into the Great Sound, he built his house which he named for the impressive naval base at Spithead in England. The year was 1790, over 200 years ago.

Hezekiah Frith's schooners came right into Turtle Bay, then much deeper, to the north of the house where they could be safely moored, and their plundered cargoes unloaded into the cellars.

In 1800, Hezekiah Frith came home with a most unique prize, a beautiful French girl whom he had carried off from the good ship "L'Augusta". Stowed away with her slave boy, Caprice, in one of the out-buildings on the Frith estate, the kidnapped beauty eventually pined away and died. Following her death Hezekiah Frith freed Caprice, according to his mistress's wishes.

This romantic episode caused a decided and regrettable rift in the family. Frith's son, young Hezekiah, lost all respect for his father, and Mrs. Frith went into decline and became a chronic invalid. The two Hezekiahs could never make amends, a tragic affair which caused the father bitter grief in his old age. Young Hezekiah died violently, struck by lightning out in Granaway Deep in 1849.

It is not surprising that eerie legends about unhappy spirits haunting Spithead persist to this day.

The ghost of the French captive was seen at one time (so she claimed) by Mrs. Eugene O'Neill, wife of the noted American dramatist whose ownership of Spithead brought fame to the house in the 1920s. During the 1950s, English playwright and lyricist, Noel Coward occupied the house immediately next door, Spithead Lodge, for a while. He admitted to having had several visitations from the long dead French girl who roamed the property, and whom he said, secretly communicated with him. His play "Blithe Spirit" was a forerunner to his later association with the 'real thing' here in Bermuda!

Spithead's present owner, Mrs. Joy Bluck Waters, has never encountered anything of an unusual nature in Spithead, but she explained that while her grandson was staying in the house recently, he awoke early one morning to find a young woman, attired in old-fashioned clothing, standing at the foot of his bed clasping a book in her hand. Not quite believing his eyes, he slowly realized she was beginning to walk away, retreating – through the wall.

Probably the strangest phenomenon was that related by one of the last descendants of Hezekiah Frith, who occupied Spithead in the 1890s. She became troubled by a nightly visitant. At nine o'clock, Frith's hour for retiring, footsteps would be heard ascending the stairs and stopping outside the bedroom door. Then the latch would lift, the door open and a shadowy figure enter. The terrified lady in the bed finally became so used to the nightly performance that she armed herself with pillows and, when the door opened she hurled them at the shadowy intruder and went to sleep!

An elderly gentleman who occupied the house in the 1950s swore on several occasions, when storms blew up out of the north at night transforming tranquil Turtle Bay into an angry sea, he would see the ghost of Hezekiah Frith restlessly pacing the wharf waiting for the wind to change so he could once again put out to sea.

On a sunny afternoon, as you drive along Harbour Road towards Somerset, you can see Spithead from a long way off. As you approach it

and get a closer view, you cannot help feeling in awe of such an impressive house which was once the proud seat of Bermuda's most prominent seafarer. Hezekiah Frith has been dead nearly 150 years but you feel such a strong presence about Spithead you would believe he was still very much alive there. I suppose he is, if you love the past. After all, that is the essence upon which all things exist.

Granaway in Warwick

built in the 1700s
All about GUESTS, REAL AND ETHEREAL . . . .
As told to Mac Musson by Carol Ashton

Granaway was a home Hezekiah Frith provided for his daughter after she was widowed by a faithless husband. Mehitabel Frith Williams overcame adversity and displayed a tremendous strength of character and spirit throughout her life; the kind of spirit that lives on. Whether the sense of warmth and caring that permeates Granaway is one that continues to reflect Mitty's former influence is not certain, but that a "presence" exists side by side with today's inhabitants has become an acceptable feature of the house.

Today, Granaway is one of Bermuda's more charming old guest houses with a special aura of timelessness guarded by walled-in gardens at the back and a gracious frontage overlooking Granaway Deep.

Carol Ashton: "Didn't I tell you about our three children down in the guest's sitting room?"

"They'd gotten hold of a Ouija Board and couldn't wait to test the performance of this alphabet toy . . . and, of course, to experience the delicious tingle and a chuckle or two that comes in anticipation of this daring venture into strange territory – they had heard about the wonders of these talking boards from their peers so why shouldn't it be fun for them too? After all, we really don't believe any of it anyway – it's a game, right?

"Dinner aside, weekend at hand, and away they go to embark on their evening's escapade with the unknown. The lower living area is cosy and comfortably appointed, with an atmosphere of long ago. The children gathered around a small table and prepared to launch themselves wholeheartedly into their most recent preoccupation.

"Hands on! – 'Is there anyone there?' – a standard and rather trite inquiry. Time passes, just enough to cause fidgeting and an odd giggle, then, their eyes, standing out like organ stops, the planchette begins to move about the board just like a hunting dog sniffing out a scent. Funny! 'Hey, you're pushing it' – 'I'm not – you are!' – 'Then it's really . . . moving by itself? . . . hey this is gre-a-t!' 'Oh, oh . . . what's that . . . .' The children tensed. Skin crawling, goosebumps on their arms, spines rigid with cold chills! As if of one accord they turned their gaze towards the doorway which stood open. The sudden intake of breath sounded the alarm. There before them stood a semi-transparent lady with long curly hair in a long white dress. She just seemed to float in front of them with a smile on her face.

"This may be a guest house alright, but right now there were – NO GUESTS! If hell could shrivel with a shriek it would've been driven from earthbound consciousness on the spot. Manners aside, they charged through the doorway and the lady without thought. The pandemonium was most admirable as the chastened children flew from this unexpected treat with a speed that would've done justice to an Olympic runner's final sprint.

"The next morning the youngsters were told to laugh at the vividness of their imaginations while the Ouija Board was unceremoniously deposited in the trash. One thing was certain, their curiosity had been satiated for the time being, but one day, it may open doors for them once again.

"It happened soon afterwards that a guest staying in the 'Strawberry Room' informed her hosts that there was a most positive presence felt there . . . she never felt alone, rather she felt a benign protectiveness prevailing about her person and always, thereafter, requested the same room for her visits."

The Moorings on Harbour Road

As told to Mac Musson by Dennis Eldridge

This is a place like Winton, in that the unseen residents enjoy teasing and engage in activities that are enough to make strong men weep. You don't have to hear the mirth from the next room, you know it's wrapping itself around you. You can feel its wry amusement as you realize you've been made to look absolutely wet – yet again! Actually, you're glad there is no one watching this one-sided one-upmanship.

The Eldridge family lived there, briefly, and recall a particular event that still evokes a sense of vague wonder. Dr. Charles Zuill is a more recent resident and his daughter assures her father that there is "something" there – probably female, because she heard the sounds of silks and taffetas rustling near her bed.

Now this is yet another house that came under the influence of old Hezekiah Frith, one way or another. Whoever it is that maintains a spiritual residency shows a leaning towards jewellery. It must be the shiny aspects that attract.

Here is the story of disappearing brilliants, in this case the engagement and wedding rings of a tenant who always very carefully placed them on top of her dresser before bathing. While dressing for a very formal evening with friends, she reached for her brush on the dresser to add the last touches to her hair and with a horrified gasp saw her rings were no longer where she had rested them.

We all can recall moments of temporary panic when our minds go blank and refuse to function on a realistic level. The time being short, and their hosts being exacting about punctuality, and knowing that the rings had to be there somewhere, they elected to look for them after they returned.

We don't have to tell you they didn't find them. They had the weekend in which to make a complete and thorough search leaving nothing to chance. When the housekeeper returned the following Monday, having gone from the "Moorings" well before the jewellery disappeared on the Friday, they enlisted her aid. They themselves were now panicking and less likely to make reliable judgements due to their very real distress. She was no more successful than they were, there was nothing to be found.

Time elapsed and the loss remained a very real fact of life. Finally the insurance company agreed to cover the loss and Dennis Eldridge advised his wife that they would depart the following weekend and take a quick run up to see the Boston jeweller and arrange for a replacement of the specially designed engagement and wedding rings as quickly as possible. With this announcement made, his wife began to relax her concern.

After her bath that evening, she went to the dresser to get her brush when, like stepping out of a time warp, there lay her two rings, exactly as she had placed them all those weeks ago. At least our "presence" had a conscience of sorts, said Mr. Eldridge!

The Deepdene

As told to Mac Musson by a taxi driver
(**also** a fountain of all knowledge)

I n the 1930s, a multi-millionaire named Blair from Far Hills, New Jersey, purchased acreage on the waterfront of Harrington Sound Road and spent months building what he hoped would be his wife's heart's desire . . . no expense was spared.

Building materials from all parts of the world were sent for; the finest wood panelling and marble, ornate fireplace mantels and intricate carvings adorned the walls. Antiques, silk brocades, paintings, Oriental carpets and finest broadlooms – nothing was overlooked.

Time passed 'til peace settled upon this perfect mansion. The dream, so long in the making, was doomed to collapse. In stunned disbelief, the husband watched his happy anticipation shatter when his wife turned her back on Deepdene Manor, hating it on sight.

It stood abandoned for years with caretakers coming and going, and when Government turned down the chance to buy it for £45,000, it finally was sold to the Hunter family and eventually was turned into a small hotel. Now a beautifully appointed condominium known as Manor House, the Deepdene of the past would certainly have lent itself to the latent possibilities of spiritual residents, since its origins were nothing if not romantic.

According to the story, no one could be sure what or who it was; the bartender, usually a fountain of all knowledge, certainly didn't know, but he, at least, gave credence to these periodic happenings and began to regularly administer a level (or shot) of "tolerance" to the ghostly suspect.

At some point it was thought that an earthbound alcoholic continued to stagger about in a spiritual stupor, nipping freely from the drinks set upon the bar at the Deepdene Boathouse Cocktail

Lounge. Many a hearty draught was heard to be quaffed, followed shortly thereafter by the sight of an empty glass where a full one had stood moments before.

It is a tad surrealistic, but try to envision the view from the Boathouse bar at night, the neighbouring lights and those of the opposite shore, giving a fairytale effect to the surrounding darkness. Imagine moonlight sparkling on the surface of the Sound broken by the luminous wake of a motorboat returning late to its moorings – tranquil and serene and, in the background of the softly lit Lounge, something vaporously insistent and otherwise invisible, guzzling down resignedly proffered alcohol – six ounces at a time! The bartender may have been suspect as to his own drinking habits, but the tale is there. Of witnesses, there are OTHER bartenders. However, if any guests were on hand when these events took place, you can be sure you'd have had difficulty in getting their personalized affirmations for others to read about.

The subject became something of a conversation piece, since a bar seems to be the most appropriate spot for spiritual assignments. Since the family that built the property were more than financially solvent, it is hard to imagine a disillusioned husband continuing to roam the halls of what had then become a hotel, forever seeking to understand his wife's total rejection of this spectacular offering and finding forgetfulness in endless Rum Swizzles – on the house!

It seems strange to gaze upon the Deepdene Boathouse, the uniqueness of its approach bridge with its picturesque tower nearby, and think back to its early beginnings. However else it has changed over the years, the boathouse tower remains oddly out of keeping with the rest of Bermudian architecture, yet quite comfortably at peace with itself. A toast to those who live and let live.

Waterfield – Hamilton Parish

As related to Mac Musson by David L. White & Sarah Dey White

Right on the water's edge at the end of My Lord's Bay sits what is today, a delightful two-level cottage overlooking Harrington Sound . . . not all that far away from Trunk Island which, we are told, has its own story. (Such is the basis for a veritable series of stories!)

Originally a small and very basic house, functional, with small "rabbit warren" rooms, it was built by the Hollis family in 1880. Eventually it was abandoned after a fire had done considerable damage, leaving only a small portion of roof intact. It had become an ideal vagrant's refuge, sitting unobtrusively at the very bottom of a large garden and grazing field. It was a dead end, in many respects!

In 1970, it was sold to David L. White by Hartwell Hollis, and thereafter underwent extensive renovations transforming it into a picturesque, architectural triumph as it nestles into the shoreline.

Enter Oscar Anderson, who was said to have been a good labourer, regular in his habits. One of these happened to be getting in the way of angry bulls, especially while they were in the heat of amorous pursuits. Who knows, perhaps he compounded the problem by wearing a red scarf around his neck!

Whatever his ill-advised tendencies, he didn't deserve to end up on the horns of this particular dilemma, but he did.

Sans the agility to avoid the infuriated bull, and lacking the necessary speed to outpace his bovine adversary, he was unceremoniously gored. Oscar Anderson, mortally wounded, succumbed to the inevitable and without ado went "through the trees" as the saying goes, amongst down-to-earth old Bermudians.

Was it his tremendous effort to seek safety that caused this supercharged atmosphere to play itself out repeatedly?

Once indoors, Oscar's footsteps are heard walking the length of the now sizeable living room, turning around, and exiting the way they came in. The door stays poised open, in anticipation of his departure then swings to and, footsteps ceasing, is once again, firmly closed.

The residents confirm that Oscar's repetitive wanderings are readily identifiable and fairly predictable . . . nor does he, for reasons unknown, ever descend to the lower level . . . maybe he's put off by the modern spiral staircase, wrought in iron that might conceivably short-circuit his etheric wanderings.

Are we looking at yet another kind of traumatized identity-crisis, did this bewildered victim of circumstance simply pass beyond life so suddenly that he returns ceaselessly, seeking to rejoin the physical body he can't recall losing?'

Sarah White, laughingly recalls the night she was relaxing in the living room, when, feeling she was being watched, she sat up slowly and casually glanced towards the windows.

Eyes were upon her! Ever was it thus! The door swung open and in a single action she flew across the room to shut it, but not before she noted the stern portion of the "intruder", its tasseled tail whipping back and forth! Its tail? Another quick look – Good God! It was a bull – looking more spirited that spiritual – surely it wasn't THE bull!

Fortunately, when she looked again, it was gone.

Shelly Hall in Shelly Bay

Related to Mac Musson by Angela Robinson during this past September, 1990

Once an imposing old dwelling built in the 19th Century, Shelly Hall is an old homestead site that today has been absorbed into new and gracious condominiums of elegant proportions.

There was a moment in the recent past when a dear friend of ours quietly admitted to having received a strong visual impression of a dignified lady of regal bearing, dressed in extremely formal and old-fashioned attire, moving silently and purposefully about the hallway of the old house. The fact that the house was empty and had been for some time, weighed heavily on our friend's awareness, especially after having examined the entire prem-ises, she found nothing to back up her initial reaction. Puzzled, she decided to say nothing for the time being and went about her business, not being too successful, however, in putting it out of her mind, where it has stayed these past few years dancing in and out of her memory. People would think she was suffering from an imagination fallout if she tried to sound others out on the matter!

Well, her impressions have been met and unknowingly observed by another, who we find is just as dubious and hesitant as she has been. This time a young tenant of the new complex, who had been playing host to two friends from the UK.

It was Angela Robinson and her fiancé who related the new circumstances, asking first in all innocence, "Has Shelly Hall ever been known for having ghosts?" Remembering our friend, we smiled encouragingly, always ready to add another event to our growing records. She went on to say that she and her fiancé had been out for the evening and returned at about 12:30 to 1:15 in the morning and, not wishing to disturb anyone, went directly to their bedroom. The following morning at break-fast, Chris, their host, said "You two got in mighty late last night."

"What do you mean by late?" we asked.

"Well, Laura and I came in after 2 a.m., and it was after that that I saw you walking down the hall towards me from the kitchen.

"Past 2 a.m.? You can't mean that, we were in bed and asleep by then."

"Can't be, we heard you in the kitchen first and then as I looked down the hall, the kitchen light was on, and you were walking toward me in the long black outfit with high neck and long sleeves. By the way, what kind of nightgown was that you were wearing, anyway?"

"Chris, we never went near the kitchen and I don't own anything black and besides its far too hot to wear anything like you're talking about – come off it, Chris, you must've seen a ghost."

Thoroughly denying such a possibility, Chris later confirmed that it was strange he had not heard the door open and close, only sounds in the kitchen. After a bit I asked him what had been there before his apartment had been built.

"Why old Shelly Hall of course," was his reply . . .

A short PS told to Joan Skinner by Betsey Outerbridge, who with her husband, Yeaton, rented the original Shelly Hall back in the 1960s. "I was walking down the hall on the ground floor of Shelly Hall, going towards the stairway upstairs, when I suddenly felt that I wasn't alone. I looked up, and saw a woman in a long gray dress with long sleeves, who silently glided by me in the hall and disappeared. I didn't feel any fear, just surprise. It was broad daylight when this happened, and I certainly have no rational explanation for what happened." The description closely matches that of the one seen in 1990.

It wouldn't do to leave this area without recounting a dreamlike incident involving "Mac and her riderless horse". This funny little tale occurred one dark summer's night in 1982.

Picturesque Radnor Road has a haunting quality at night, eerily enhanced by a sparcity of street lamps. Trees, houses, open fields and, when it's late, a lot of silence. Having left a friend's home at a still respectable hour, serene in the knowledge that I was the only designated driver in sight, I was driving with great care, only my headlights illuminating the narrow winding road ahead. The resultant shadows were dense and black on either side, and all was quiet save for the car's muted engine.

Out of nowhere, breathtaking in its suddeness, loomed the large, dark, riderless horse, galloping at full speed directly into the path of the car. Collision with this ghostly silhouette vividly outlined by the headlamps was imminent. I jammed on my brakes, shutting my eyes tight and simultaneously waiting for the impact that could not possibly be avoided.

Silence! Utter and complete, accompanied the cessation of all movement. Car, horse and me – all as still as the night – not a sound. Not the faintest suggestion of a horse's hoofs cantering off into the distance – nothing. Even the car had stalled.

It was several years before I fully accepted the slow-to-emerge realization, that it was not my expertise at the wheel that had spared the horse – the horse simply wasn't there to hit . . . not in 1982, that is.

Tamarisk Hall

As told to Joan Skinner by Johnny and Bill Outerbridge

From the Royal Gazette, August 8th, 1978
Sub-titled – "A friendly ghost on the edge of Hamilton"

Bermuda is believed to have its share of ghosts, but getting people to talk about them is not so easy.

There is one professional man, however, who readily admits to harbouring a friendly ghost – and of all places, in an old house on the edge of busy Hamilton. The roar of traffic within a few yards of gracious Tamarisk Hall does not deter an old lady, long gone from this world, from pacing its rooms by night.

Dr. William "Peter" Outerbridge, who has his dental office in the historic residence, with its garden surroundings, will miss the gentle ghost when he moves elsewhere after the house is sold. She is not the reason for his planning to leave it, he stresses.

"I've been extremely happy here," he said. "I do have a ghost, but it has nothing to do with the office. It's because of planning regulations that I decided I had to sell the house in order to acquire another office.".

Neither does the ghost have anything to do with the late Mrs. Stella Halsall, who died in Tamarisk Hall in May 1970, after many years of residence.

Dr. Outerbridge does not know the exact identity of the spectre, but understands from the old-timers familiar with the history of the house, that it must be an old lady who died of emphysema in the house after living there for a number of years.

"She manifests herself with heavy breathing as she walks around," he said. "We knew of her before we moved in. She is an extremely friendly type of individual and has never been any cause of concern.

"She sort of walks around one end of the house, primarily at night. We have never seen her, but only heard her. The children, who sleep in that end, could probably tell you more about her, but they are in Canada until the Christmas holidays."

Johnny Outerbridge:
"I came home for the summer holiday the year we bought Tamarisk Hall. My father, Peter, enjoys all the aspects of construction, so he was doing most of the renovations to the house himself. One very still, very hot summer night, we were painting in the living room. My father, being a practical man, had only one light going in the room, so we were both working very close together, near the front door. Now the front door is a very old and heavy cedar Dutch door, with heavy brass fittings. And on this windless night, it suddenly closed. Not with the slam as though wind had snapped it shut, but very deliberately; first the bottom half, and then the top half.

"Peter put a small tin of paint thinner in front of the door, for surely, on such a windless night, that is all that would be required to hold the door open. Again the door was shut just as firmly as before. A gallon paint tin was then placed in front of the newly-opened door, and we watched in amazement as the door slowly pushed the container out of its way to close again. The two of us beat a hasty retreat.

"One of Dad's helpers, Bookie Hall, a very fine carpenter, would not stay at the site after dark. 'I hear my wife calling', he would say, and gone him!

"As I look back now, I can't imagine why I was not frightened or slightly awed by these goings-on, but, at the time, I was in my middle teens, and these were just 'things' that happened. Evidently the old lady liked the front door closed during the day, and the dining room door open, probably to clear out the stale air from long-ago cigar or pipe smoke from the night before. I can remember sitting under a table in the living room with my friend, John Lindsay, and watching the doors open and close. We just looked on the whole thing as very funny. We'd open the door; it would close. We'd close the other door and it would open. Except one day the dining room door opened and someone walked through it! It was my sister, Janice, but for some minutes there we were somewhat alarmed!

"My bedroom had a bathroom en suite, and this was where I would sneak my cigarettes. I would be able to hear footsteps as they came down the living room in time to douse my forbidden indulgence, leap out of the bathroom, and greet whoever was coming to my room, hoping they wouldn't smell the smoke!

"Very often, however, though I heard footsteps, there would be no one there. And I soon began to realize that, if the footsteps were accompanied by the sound of bric-a-brac jiggling on the Dutch cupboard which stood against the living room wall, there would be a body to go with them. If the footsteps were heard only by themselves, there would be no one. And I still wasn't frightened. That was just the way things were.

"One night my parents had some friends over for dinner. It was winter, when we used to have a winter, near Christmas, the windows all closed and a fire in the fireplace. The talk turned to the house and ghosts, and there was much scoffing at the idea of any hauntings. Suddenly, all the Christmas cards, which had been strung around the room, were tossed and turned in the air and slowly fell to the floor – a snowstorm of Christmas greetings. This caused much consternation, only to be outdone by a large mahogany curtain rod crashing to the floor, right next to the couch, pulling with it the large screws and 6" cedar dowels which had attached it to the wall. The dinner party ended rather abruptly.

"An interesting bit of history. The only person ever to be sentenced to burn at the stake in Bermuda, was Sally Bassett, on a charge of Petit Treason. The magistrate who sentenced her was my ancestor, William Outerbridge, and it was on the very grounds where Tamarisk Hall now stands, that she was burned at the stake. My father is also William Outerbridge, as is my brother."

And a few experiences from Bill Outerbridge.

"When my brother, John, and I were away at school, the bedroom, which we shared when we were home, became the guest bedroom. But, without exception, guests would only stay in that room one night and would then move into the family room and sleep on the couch. And all this with no prior knowledge of any ghostly happenings. I mean, you don't ask your houseguests to go and sleep in the haunted room!

"My Grandmother, Grammy, came to visit, a strict Presbyterian from Canada, who neither drank nor smoked. One evening she looked up at the doorway to see a figure standing there. Thinking it was her daughter, Jean, she proceeded to start a conversation with her, and, upon getting no response, looked to the doorway again, only to see that it was now empty. I figured that if a God-fearing person like my Grammy saw something, there was definitely something there!

"My most frightening experience happened about three o'clock one morning. I awoke to hear this very heavy breathing, and thought to myself, 'I really should give up smoking!' I slowed my breathing, eventually holding my breath, but this heavy breathing continued. It was in the bed; in my pillow! I shot up in bed and snapped on the bedside light, but there was nothing there. I told my folks about it the following morning. They told me that one of the things they had noticed while reno-vating the house was the sound of heavy breathing coming from that bedroom, but at the time attrib-uted it to the wind sighing in the trees.

"My brother John and I would often at night hear the floorboards creaking, the sound moving from north to south. And many times, in the morning, we'd even jump on the floorboards in the area trying to make something creak, but couldn't. Many nights I'd lie in bed and mentally plead with the ghost not to show himself because I'd probably die of a heart attack.

Footnotes from Johnny.

"I was asked to house-sit Caledonia, in St. George's, while the tenants were away. This is a large house at the top of Barrack Hill, with a two-story turret on the top. The woman of the house made up the bedroom in the turret for me to use during my stay. But I could not bring myself to use it. I spent the entire house-sit sleeping on the living room couch. One morning, I awoke to see three children skipping down the steps going to the second story. They seemed to be leaving for school, holding books, straightening their clothes and laughing. As I watched, they just disappeared. Kind of faded.

"I also had a very moving experience when my Bermuda grandmother, Alla, died. She was in the hospital, having seemingly fallen into a deep sleep from which no one could waken her. We had all visited her at the hospital, talking to her, trying to awaken her, but meeting with very limited response. A nod, perhaps, a slight shaking of the head. The monitors, to which she was attached, all indicated a good heartbeat and positive vital signs. Suddenly, though, the monitors showed no change, my Aunt Barbara looked at Alla and said, 'She's gone.'

"At that very moment, I was painting a house in Tucker's Town. Suddenly, I felt the presence of a person, though I could see no one, and felt a gentle patting on my arm. I know it was Alla. I burst into tears, wishing I could have been at the hospital at the last. The owner of the house came to comfort me, and asked me what was wrong.

"'My Grandmother just died,' I said. Her amazement at this announcement did a little to lighten my grief."

Patricia and Gary Phillips, present owners, and contented residents of Tamarisk Hall, find it to be friendly albiet a bit draghty. Visitors would remark on the feeling of a very definite 'presence' in the house, but in every instance, the feeling was comfortable rather than threatening.

A 'Bermuda Cottage' in Somerset

by Chris and Karen Lusher as told to Joan Skinner

This charmingly restored old Bermuda cottage, circa 1720, sits atop a hill over-looking the sleepy village of Somerset, with views of the ocean stretching to the horizon. This is the Lusher's account of the events that took place since their taking possession of the house.

The ghost appears to be a Mrs. King.

"We had not noticed any untoward happenings, except a feeling of warmth about the cottage. A very happy, contented feeling. But when we started our renovations, a presence very definitely made itself known. The first instance occurred when we were working on the small children's room at the back of the house. I had a Jamaican helper who came out of the room and said, 'Hey, mon, you got a lady sittin' in the corner!' In disbelief I asked him to describe her, and he said that she was wearing bedroom slippers, a robe, a black shawl, and was smoking a cigarette! We went to investigate, and saw nothing, but were assured by my friend that, 'We Jamaicans are very ghost aware.'

"I got in touch with the daughter and granddaughters of a Mrs. King, who had been an earlier inhabitant of the house, and when I described what my friend has seen, they said, "That's Nana.'

"The daughter and granddaughters came to the house one evening to see if they could make any contact with Nana. We were standing on the upper floor of the of the house, looking down through the joists to the small room below. We had yet to put the planks down over the joists. The assembled relatives then called out, 'Nana, if you're here open and close the door.' To our amazement, this happened about three times. They then said, 'now open the door wide, and slam it.' When this happened, I raced down the stairs to find that the door was still securely bolted!

"One evening, I was tiling the downstairs room with my friend, Michael Hooper. As the planks still had to be put down, you could see the joists to the upper level. Suddenly, Michael said 'There's someone watching us.' I looked up and saw nothing except what I thought was a shadow moving. I said to Michael not to worry, it was only Mrs. King. And then, jokingly, I thought, I called out, 'Mrs.

King, if you're here, turn on the hall light upstairs,' and on it came. I then asked her to turn it off, and off it went. I have never seen anyone leave a place as fast as Michael did!

"Another time, I was on the ladder, painting in between the beamed ceiling. There was a "live" wire dangling down where the chandelier was going to be, and my elbow brushed the wire. The shock I got made me dizzy, and I started to fall backwards off the ladder. And then, it was just as if a hand pushed me back up on the ladder. Weird. But I did remember to say, 'Thank you, Mrs. King!'

Karen was telling me that their silverware goes missing all the time. "I think we're down to about three forks and two spoons." She said she used to blame it on Chris and the kids, but the amount of cutlery that would disappear couldn't be accounted for that way. And, never knives – only forks and spoons.

"The story goes', said Karen, 'that Mrs. King was expecting her entire family for brunch on the day she died, so maybe she's still setting the table!"

Windswept Cottage
on the grounds of Cambridge Beaches
Adapted from a Bermuda News Bureau release by S. Day

The story is one of the oldest in the world – one of many Bermuda Triangles. The gentleman, Hugh Gray, was a youthful spirit, a gay blade who, it is said, paved the way for the establishment of this well known guest colony in the early 1920s and met a dramatic end several years later.

His marriage, for all his boyish charm, suffered estrangement due to his young wife's pre-occupation with the police commissioner.

Here enters the tale of suspicion, jealousy, intrigue and murder.

Hugh Gray, who always enjoyed a day on the water, arranged a night-outing for his wife and their law-enforcement officer-friend, with himself at the helm. An innocent enough way to spend a beautiful summer's evening. And what is more natural than a threesome taking a leisurely sail under a cloudless night sky at the end of a hot and sultry day?

It was said that, out of nowhere, had come a brief and sudden storm that swamped their boat and overwhelmed them, but, whatever the actual cause, it was a wet and exhausted Hugh Gray who finally returned to shore, alone.

Village gossip had already been having a field day at Hugh Gray's expense, but failed to notice his growing distress and occasional terseness when spoken to. Now, with the loss of his wife and the police commissioner, whispers ran rife. With the nightmare of events that followed, rumour-mongers began to tie one on with a vengeance! More than mere broad hints outlined not only a motive, but a devilish plan of premeditated murder.

The commissioner's body was discovered a few days later, caught on a reef, but the wife was never seen again. Foul play seemed almost certain – but couldn't be proved.

Years later, an old bartender known as "C.B." told the tale of Hugh Gray many times over, never altering or embellishing the facts as he knew them, and in concluding the melodramatic details, in hushed tones, he would end the saga:

"He met his end by mysterious hands", having been found dead at the foot of his narrow stairs at Windswept Cottage, neck broken, alone and unattended.

Justice had prevailed – better still, Hugh Gray's sudden demise had all the satisfying appearances of a supernatural vengeance.

King's Point

in Mangrove Bay
As related to Mac Musson by Edna & Teddy Tucker

King's Point is the home of Teddy Tucker, internationally known for his underwater ventures, knowledge of the sea, and many successful treasure dives around the reefs of Bermuda, and his wife Edna, who is gracious hostess and friend to an endless parade of guests from all around the world.

Out on the point overlooking the turquoise brilliance of Mangrove Bay, stands an old homestead with an interesting past and fascinating present, couched in mysteries of the sea . . . here is the home of two wonderfully in-tune people whose lives intermingle with the ghosts of the deep, and the seductive Lorelie of the reefs. Within the wooded privacy that surrounds the house, time recalls in its stillness the tragedy of a disturbed suicide whilst the household itself contains entities who all but pull up a chair at the kitchen table when company is present.

Now, an animal's sixth sense is seldom questioned, and in the area of the unseen, their ability to see is remarkable. Shortly after moving into King's Point, the Tucker's standard schnauzer, Mitzie, introduced them to the reality of their newly acquired resident ghost. Not that Mitzie objected to it's existence so much – rather it was the on-again, off-again quality of this uncalled-for entity that must have annoyed her. All set for a good display of raised hackles and guttural snarls, the visitation seemingly departed without a fight. If it would stick around long enough the uneven relationship might be resolved, after all that's a lot of steam to get up for nothing!

"Looks like we have a ghost around here!" was Edna's laughing observation.

History points to a sad and jilted suitor who, in his disgruntled vexations, paid a final honour to the maiden of his choice. Unable to face her rejection of his proposal, he hung himself on an overhanging branch in the woodlands behind King's Point. It is believed to be his mortal remains that are buried nearby, there to rest for all eternity. Whether the fair young maiden was suitably impressed by this dramatic exit and how she directed her life thereafter, is not known, but it doesn't appear that her phantom is pacing the woods in perpetual or even periodic remorse.

Today, it is only the tragic young man of yesteryear who trips through the door, crosses the living room and sits firmly on the antique brocade sofa. He seems agitated as if waiting for someone or something. His attire is of the early 1700s and none too clean. He disappears only to repeat the performance over and over again through the years. On one occasion Edna decided on a move that would trick either her senses or those of the etheric guest – she moved the furniture! Chairs and tables were shifted and the sofa was transferred to an entirely different wall, opposite the ritual path. In due course "he" arrived and with the briefest of pauses, did a deft turn and settled onto his sofa as usual.

Makes one wonder if the antique sofa itself was the source of the haunting, rather than the house.

Fun and games abound here. The flesh and the spirit are separate on the one hand and as one on the other. Edna prepares meals and cooks alongside an unseen "helper" who turns on taps and fills glasses, splashing, gurgling – a trickling, giggly, sort of experience, for the eyes see nought, only the ears tell all.

The atmosphere around us that contains its own recall through time can be selective and, if an area is alive with past happenings, there is no limit to the variety of manifestations. King's Point has all the recognized senses covered in their turn – sight, sound, touch, a moment when a visitor thought her host or hostess had tapped her shoulder to get her attention only to find herself quite a distance away from the others in the group, and, finally – smell. The latter presents itself in the aroma of roast beef, pungent, and mouthwatering, coming from an empty kitchen at 3 o'clock in the morning when all hands are trying to sleep! Investigation does not serve the palate a longed for slice of satisfaction – there is simply nothing to be found.

When glass breaks in this house during the night, it shatters. The sound depicts an entire cabinet full of stemware and brandy snifters being smashed in the hallway. The great thing is, you don't have to clean it up the next morning!

The initial "dry-run" of this alarming special effect was delivered in the middle of the night shortly after the Tuckers had first settled in. The unmistakable smash and tinkle of quantities of crystal caused Edna to sit up straight in her bed, thinking the cats had run amok!

Teddy Tucker, partially awake and alerted to the alternatives by Edna, elected to face the resultant mess in the morning. This was just as well, since the event was to be repeated regularly over the years to follow, while the crystal in question, remains intact, and as useful as ever today.

It is said that during the 1800s, a distraught mother drowned in a desperate attempt to rescue her young daughter who had toddled to the edge of the small dock and fallen into the water. At one point inside the house one gets a sense of an emotional tension still suspended in the atmosphere. Whether this poor woman, in her terror and haste, dropped a tray of crystal as she ran out the door in a vain bid to save her child, is at least something to ponder.

Edna Tucker recalls with some amusement, a young house guest built like Arnold Schwarzenagger, who slept like a tender babe in arms when visiting King's Point, "but absolutely refused to turn the lights out all night long!" Edna and Teddy finally ventured to suggest he might sleep more restfully with the lights out. He responded with feeling, "Dammit Tuckers – not in THIS house!"

Salthaven in Devonshire

by John Cox

Standing like a sentry at the mouth of Devonshire Dock, Salthaven remains something of an enigma. Nobody is certain when the house was built or, indeed, who even lived there in the beginning. Various families engaged in fishing and shipbuilding occupied the house through the 19th century. In the 1820s, Elias Tynes and his wife, Affliction, were living there. Elias was lost at sea in a wrecking expedition in the Bahamas in 1833. Fate saw that his poor widow was well named!

In 1977, I visited the house as a guest of David and Mary Margaret Dill, who were staying there at the time. It was a stormy winter night, and the northwest gales dashed angry waves against the house.

"It's not unusual to arrive home and find the living room and kitchen flooded with sea water," remarked Mary Margaret, as we all glanced across the room at the shuttered windows, half expecting the sea to break through at any moment. "In a hurricane, the sea actually breaks right over the roof," claimed David. "It's very dramatic!" My only consolation was that hurricane season was a long way off. The storm outside was trial enough.

"Do you have any ghosts?" I asked. David and Mary Margaret looked at one another.

"Of course," answered David. "Tell John about it, Mary Margaret."

Mary Margaret turned her head towards the stair well. "It lives upstairs," she started.

"We think it's a woman. We've never seen it, but we hear it, or should I say her, all the time. She sings laments. They're old-fashioned tunes, reminiscent of the ones of long ago. Actually, it only happens when we're here by ourselves. At first it unnerved us, but eventually we got used to it, and now we even enjoy it. It's always upstairs, never anywhere else in the house."

I wondered whether the wind had caused what could have been mistaken for a human, singing. The question did not fare well with my hostess. "Never!" came the assertive reply. "Do you think you'd hear soft singing sounds with all that commotion going on, the banging and the crashing?! No, we hear it when it's dead calm." It soon became clear that these strange encounters had to be of a supernatural nature.

Some months later, on a still, summer evening, I once again found myself a guest at Salthaven. What seemed an almost eerie contrast to my first visit, when we were huddled against a storm in the living room, on this occasion we sat on the verandah overlooking the North Shore, watching the sun go down while the water gently lapped the shoreline. The scene made me remember those timeless lines by Zen:

ince well I know that everything
ich seems real is not so,
ust I also know — dreams are
t dreams?"

The sea has her mysteries, countless as they are timeless, and they belong to her alone. Every so often however, she offers a tantalizing glimpse into the wonders stored within her depths. From these subaqueous regions rises a brief and tenuous reality which, if observed, leaves the viewer a trifle bemused, for as the vision appears, teasing the senses, it as quickly dissolves into the time-warp from which it emerged. Who could possibly confuse the legendary islands of long ago with the Bermuda of today? Well certainly not our present day businessman, accustomed to the faster pace of today's marketing strategies. Such fanciful imaginings bring us to . . . .

Frick's Point, Tucker's Town

As told to Mac Musson by George Morris

Here we were, a banking officer, a police sergeant, and a longshoreman – all down-to-earth, no-nonsense individuals who enjoy, along with their weekend relaxation, some serious fishing, in the interests of well-stocked freezers.

"This incident records a not very unusual bone fishing trip just like hundreds of other excursions. Not as fishy as it may sound, but whilst the catch was the objective, what we got was a tale we were hesitant to tell, since like the biggest proverbial catch of the day . . . the lady got away! Talk about feeling foolish!

"It was dusk and the early evening perfect for bone fishing in the shallows between Castle Island and the Point. The sea was so still, with not the slightest breath of air to ripple its surface. We waded over to a large rock to settle down to the task at hand when Sgt. Nobby Clark, true to his profession, pointed to some small footprints clearly stamped in the damp sand, moving down from the rock we sat on, and going purposefully along the shoreline. There was no sign of them arriving – just leaving, as if they'd come out of the sea itself.

"They appeared to be prints from pointed shoes with a little high heel. As of one accord, we jumped onto the beach and, for a short distance, followed the path of footprints. Suddenly we stood stock-still and looked ahead – there she was, luminous – her floating gray-white cloak draped grace-fully from her shoulders and wearing a bonnet of sorts, a woman in Colonial attire, standing in watchful silence. She seemed totally unaware of our puzzled attention. She was standing on the sandy rise near the old tower, the distance between us being little more than 25 feet when, without further ado, she gracefully and noiselessly faded away – drifting out of our lives as easily as she walked in. There was nowhere for her to go, but she went anyway, as easy as one-two-three! And she took her footprints with her! Not a sign of them leading away – nothing!

"It's not difficult to imagine the scenario as we three die-hards watched this eerie, and suspiciously spectral-like replay, enfold before us, slowly turning to one another for the comfort of corroboration of the senses. This shared observation was in no way accountable by any ordinary means.

"Nobby Clark, satisfied that he had been witness to something out of this world, had only one thing to say – 'Well friends, I'm out of here!' and he went.

"Come to think of it, the rest of us weren't far behind!"

Why this intriguing appearance and disappearance, this phantasm of the past rising out of the edge of the sea? Was it to search the sands for something left behind, or was it someone searching the horizon for the return of a loved one? To this day they have no idea. A woman with no apparent past and certainly no future! Never saw anything like that before – or since! Beached, bothered, and not a little bewildered, were they!

Bermuda's shores, like many other seaport islands will always be awash with spiritual debris, littered with an invisible life force that has, over the centuries, shed its mortality on one or several of our reefs. This began long before our early settlers put their roots down, giving these islands their present identity by fair means or foul.

Wreck Hill was once the site of false beacons and the earlier days of home-brewed piracy where even the local Padré, at the helm of his congregation, was known to halt the service in the interests of rescuing a newly foundered merchantman. After all who would question the motives of a man of God?

Sometimes however, it was an unanticipated and therefore unusual visitation that drew the attention of the inhabitants of Sandys Parish.

The Eliza Ann
Revised by Mac Musson from Sister Jean Kennedy's "Bermuda Hodge Podge"

In 1833 a derelict schooner was observed by a lone fisherman, drifting aimlessly towards Daniel's Head. Fully rigged, this 60 foot vessel stood off the Island with dignity, as silent as a tomb. Getting no response to his hail, the fisherman approached with caution and obvious purpose – a prize for the taking? He boarded with speed only to be met by a most astonishing sight – all hands were there to meet him, but it was a skeleton crew in the purest sense. Clothing still draped the individuals of this macabre tableau, miming a nautical reception committee. The bewildered fisherman made a hasty retreat to bring a number of men to lend a hand and sail the Eliza Ann into Ely's Harbour.

Only her non-perishable cargo was intact, which bespoke many months drifting aimlessly, a plaything of tides and currents. Labels, jewellery and a scholastic medallion gave the salvagers a clue to her origins and, through advertising in American newspapers, the ship's owner was eventually located.

It was learned that the Eliza Ann had sailed out of Boston's Mystic Harbour nearly a year before. There was never an explanation as to why a well-appointed ship, with ample stores and water, should be a floating funeral barge for a full complement of hands amongst whom were the two sons of the owner and his nephew, who had been the Eliza Ann's Master.

They didn't know about the Bermuda Triangle!

The Minerva

As related to Mac Musson by Colin Hind

Here is a tale of far more incredible proportions. The Minerva was built on the North Shore in Bermuda, early in the 19th Century. She had developed an enviable mercantile reputation by the time she left Ely's Harbour under full sail in 1849, her destination Africa and the Far East. After two years had passed without a sign of her returning, she was presumed lost.

It was, therefore, a startled community surrounding Ely's Harbour that awoke one morning to see this nearly forgotten ship, forlorn, and listing heavily, in the lagoon that seemed to embrace her – a ghost ship to all intents and purposes. Of the crew, there was no trace. No Flying Dutchman this, the Minerva played no phantom games shimmering into and out of haze. The last entry in the ship's log placed her far out in the Atlantic, possibly as far as the Indian Ocean where, in danger of foundering, she was abandoned at sea. With not a soul on board, she had drifted at the will of the ocean currents for more than 14 months!

Navigation of these reef bound waters, and the narrow inlet into the harbour itself, is a task for only the most experienced helmsmen. For the Minerva to have drifted in without assistance, sails shredded and flapping, rudder running free, is a story of incredible dimensions. Only her ship's log found in the Captain's quarters gave mute testimony to the awesome time lapse noted in its last entry all that time ago. Even this gave no hint at what might have actually taken place.

Seaworthy she may have been, but few would have wished to trust themselves to her future. Presumably, she was dispatched under tow to an outside agency, which might have felt less superstition on behalf of an unsuspecting crew yet to be pressed into service on this "ghost" ship.

Heraclitus 500 BC
"Because it is so unbelievable, the truth escapes becoming known."

Hold that thought 'til we meet again!

99

Printed in the United States
1398341V00005BD/87/P